MARCH
of the
SUFFRAGETTES

MARCH of the SUFFRAGETTES

Rosalie Gardiner Jones and the March for Voting Rights

by **ZACHARY MICHAEL JACK**

ZEST BOOKS

To my New York family of the Now—
Tasha, Henry and Ezra—
and my New York family of the Then,
Levi, Sally, Eliza, William, and Ben

& most of all

To that intrepid general,
and incomparable suffragette,
Rosalie Gardiner Jones

Connect with Zest!

- zestbooks.net/blog   - twitter.com/zestbooks
- zestbooks.net/contests   - facebook.com/BooksWithATwist

2443 Fillmore Street, Suite 340, San Francisco, CA 94115 | www.zestbooks.net

TABLE OF CONTENTS

INTRODUCTION:
WOMEN OF ACTION

Have you ever wanted something so badly you were willing to go an incredible distance for it?

Not so very long ago, a "platoon" of remarkable young women did just that. They marched hundreds of miles for their cause, fighting not just Mother Nature (in the form of wind, fog, sleet, snow, mud, and ice), but also overprotective parents, male and female hecklers, escaped convicts, and corrupt millionaires. They formed an army, classifying themselves as generals, surgeon generals, colonels, corporals, and privates, while cooking up marching songs to buoy their spirits.

These intrepid young women walked the line for something called suffrage — a constitutionally guaranteed right to vote. Once achieved, it meant that American lawmakers would never again be able to deny women a say in who governed them and how. By modern standards the cause of Rosalie Gardiner Jones and her band of marching suffragettes constituted a very basic request, and yet their ultimate goal sometimes seemed to them as insurmountable as the formidable hills and valleys that lay between them and the politicians they desperately hoped to convince.

In the late autumn of 1912 Rosalie Jones got a big idea from her sister suffragettes in England, who had undertaken suffrage hikes in an attempt to secure equal rights. Rosalie believed that her American sisters in suffrage could pull off their own long march. Now she needed to convince others of her belief.

She could, and she did, use anger as an asset, shouting her beliefs to everyone and anyone who would listen. But that didn't work, as it seldom does. There were plenty of people then, as now, that didn't like the sound of a woman's voice making angry demands. Frustrated, Rosalie thought for a time that she might go at it alone — who needed timid and aged suffragists anyway? But that strategy didn't work out very well for her either. If one wanted to make a big change in society, one needed the help and support of others. By age twenty-eight Rosalie Jones had come to accept that fact.

So the youthful Miss Jones got involved in "the system" despite her reservations about the way it worked, or didn't. First she joined the Women's Suffrage Party of New York, and very shortly thereafter she became the district leader of her county. As a district leader Rosalie found that people who before seemed not to give her the time of day began to listen, so when she came before the committee one day in 1912 with a bold idea, she won their endorsement and support.

Rosalie Gardiner Jones was a can-do girl; that's how she earned her nickname of "General." She had graduated college by 1912, and pictures of the time showed that she could not only drive her own car but also repair its tires when inevitably they went flat. She was a suffragette through and through, one who believed women ought to be trusted to do by and for themselves. That was especially true — or ought to have been true — when it came to voting, except that in New York and most other states in December of 1912 women were prevented from voting, and that was an injustice worth fighting against tooth and nail.

Rosalie's parents were wealthy New Yorkers, but she was far from a wallflower. Her mother was described as a "bitter anti-suffragist," otherwise known as an "Anti," which meant that Rosalie would have to defy her influential mother, becoming, in effect, what her mother most ardently resisted. This fact alone would be enough to daunt any ordinary daughter, but General Jones knew that she must lose many things and many people if she hoped to gain a larger victory. It was a daughter's duty to follow her own heart and her own passion wherever they might lead, just as it was a mother's duty to try to safeguard her daughter's well-being.

By the time she reached her twenties Rosalie had come to believe in an active, boots-on-the-ground variety of protest, as opposed to more shopworn versions of the suffrage movement, which called to mind well-to-do older ladies making pretty speeches that got few results. Thus the General's first step was to find out who was a fair-weather supporter of equal voting rights for women and who, by contrast, could be counted on to "vote with their feet" for their cause come rain or come shine.

Rosalie's idea was as simple as it was bold. What if she formed an all-women army and walked — yes, walked — from Broadway in New York City all the way to the state capital, where she proposed to present a petition for women's rights to Governor-elect William Sulzer of New York? She planned to call her co-adventurers "pilgrims" because they would be walking for a sacred cause. More often than not, reporters called the more demonstrative, boots-on-the-ground activists like Rosalie Jones "suffragettes" rather than "suffragists." *Suffragettes* got things done!

Rosalie's idea, like many ideas that ultimately catch on, possessed built-in appeal. Her suffrage hike would be dramatic, of that there was little doubt. It would be physically, emotionally, and intellectually challenging, and that, too, was important, since it was these very traits that many anti-suffragists, men chief among them, claimed that women naturally lacked. And finally Rosalie's proposed march would be eminently newsworthy. In order to win the vote for women, Rosalie and her troops knew they must first convince the good people of America reading the evening newspaper at home in their living rooms.

December 1912 seems like a long time ago, but for the most part these young and daring activists led lives very much like our own. In 1912 there were cars on the road, telephones in homes, and record players in living rooms. Commercial refrigeration had been around for nearly three quarters of a century, and the government had begun making radio broadcasts. Olympic-class luxury ocean liners plied the Atlantic between America, Europe, and Britain, including one especially ill-fated super-ship called the RMS *Titanic*, which had sunk earlier that same year.

And yet for all these modern conveniences there were still plenty of frankly silly things young women weren't supposed to do in 1912. Some of these prohibitions were really quite ridiculous, including no-nos like whistling in the street, owning dogs, and riding bicycles. There were of course a handful of individual states where a woman could exercise her right to "enfranchisement" even back then, but there were nearly four times as many more where she could not cast her ballot, and the United States Constitution still refused provision for her voting alongside her husband, brothers, and male friends. This was an intolerable situation for progressive young women who had grown up believing they could, and indeed should, do anything a man could do.

An unusual number of these empowered young women lived in New York, the state that had hosted the first and most famous women's rights convention on two very warm July days in 1848 in Seneca Falls. It was at the Seneca Falls Convention, as it came to be called, at which the right to vote became the single most cherished political goal for women of the day. Elizabeth Cady Stanton, who some called the mother of the suffragist movement, had helped write a Declaration of Sentiments for the convention, patterning her document on the Declaration of Independence while adding the word *women*, as in "all men and women are created equal," to her resolutions wherever and whenever the term applied. At the convention Stanton introduced even more resolutions, including one that read, "It is the duty of the women of this country to secure to themselves their sacred right to the elective franchise."

Still, nearly sixty-five years later in December of 1912, as Rosalie and her women's army prepared to set off on their impossible journey, the women of New York had not yet won the vote. This unthinkable delay had become a source of great and gathering frustration. In the years between 1848 and 1912 enterprising women would gather together with lofty goals and high aspirations, and drawing strength from one another as well as from their shared cause, they would ask for reasonable things that only seemed extravagant to the men in their lives. And then, of course, nothing would happen — or more accurately, very little would happen — so little, in fact, that a casual observer might think no progress had been made at all.

History moved more slowly then; its great wheel took longer to turn in those days before Facebook and the Internet. It wasn't that nothing happened; great inventions happened, wars happened, presidential assassinations happened, but these happenings seemed mostly the cause and concern of men. But what better time to go about asking for such

"General" Rosalie Jones

a change than at Christmastime — December — the one month of the year where it was okay, and even expected, to wish for the improbable.

The young women who dreamed of earning the right to vote in the days leading up to that Christmas of 1912 weren't ordinary wishers any more than they were ordinary women. Ordinary wishes were idle hopes that might or might not come true, depending. No, these young suffragettes were not the kind to allow themselves wishes unless those wishes could be put into dramatic action.

The suffrage hike to the capital would demand all of their intelligence and ingenuity. Along the way Rosalie Jones and the officers in her makeshift army would face many obstacles, crises, and mysteries. For example, not long after the brave pilgrims set forth from Broadway, two manhunts were underway in the rugged terrain along their route.

The first was for millionaire businessman William Rockefeller, who had escaped a Congressional summons by, it was presumed, disappearing into the Adirondacks earlier that summer. By December of 1912 Sergeant-at-Arms Charles S. Riddell and two deputies had grown desperate to find him, hunting up and down the hills and vales of central New York to find the famous businessman believed to be hiding out in the snowbound forests. At the same time that William Rockefeller remained at large, one of New York's most notorious criminals, Chester "Kid" Yates, had recently escaped from the infamous Sing-Sing prison under cover of a heavy fog.

Along the way Rosalie's "trampers" would face snow, wind, rain, and ice. They would meet and mingle with the rich and famous—Astors and Rockefellers and Vanderbilts—and attend glamorous balls and high teas with high-society suffragists, but they would also eat at the side of the road and thrill to the sound of wild animals in the adjacent woods. They would fight blisters and swollen feet and bone-chilling cold. They would compose and sing their own marching songs to keep their spirits up, even as differences among them threatened to tear them apart.

They would experience good times and tragic times along their route and thereafter: life and love, to be sure, but also disloyalty and disillusionment. They would be cheered and jeered, at once blessed by acts of great kindness and victimized by acts of prejudice. They would see their marching armies reduced to three tired pilgrims and swell to lines of followers as long as two city blocks.

But before any of this could happen, these women, young and old, would have to do as all brave heroes have done before and since. On the morning of December 16, they would have to take their first steps.

CHAPTER 1:
FIRST STEPS

It was Sunday, December 8, an otherwise ordinary day of rest for Rosalie Gardiner Jones — that is, until an idea that had been simmering inside Rosalie privately for several weeks sent her running to the telephone to call her good friend Ida Craft. When Ida answered, the words tumbled so quickly from Rosalie's mouth that Ida had to ask her friend to start again from the beginning.

Both Rosalie and Ida wanted to vote in their state's and nation's elections more than anything else in the world, but to make that happen they needed to do something dramatic, Rosalie believed, to draw the nation's attention to the righteousness of their beliefs.

What if they formed a suffragette army and hiked a great distance, Rosalie suggested, making persuasive speeches along the way.

How far would they go, Ida asked in return, and who in heaven's name would march along with them?

These were harder questions to answer. Rosalie had worked for the women's vote before, including the previous summer when she'd pulled a yellow pony cart — a vehicle that had been in the family for generations — for miles in an effort to convince her family's neighbors on Long Island of the necessity of women's suffrage.

She had marched in Ohio as well, where the votes-for-women cause had been roundly defeated. Throughout that summer and right up until the day of the vote on September 3, they had posted signs and placards with messages like "Give the women a square deal" and "Come in and learn why women ought to vote."[1] Rosalie and her allies ultimately tasted bitter defeat in the Buckeye State, but the setback there had only served to motivate them further. Two months later, at the national suffrage convention in Philadelphia in November, came the first inklings of the idea Rosalie now dared broach with Ida.

On the other end of the telephone, Ida stood waiting for answers, trying to hide her growing excitement as Rosalie laid out a daring plan for a suffrage march of nearly two hundred miles.[2]

The truth was Rosalie didn't have any idea how many other people — if any — would be willing to march with them. Even she and Ida had a hard time imagining forsaking a Christmas holiday spent at home with their families and friends.

And then there was the issue of Rosalie's family. The Joneses of Long Island were well-to-do and well-known, and while this was an advantage, it could also prove something of a cross to bear.[3] Whenever a young woman like Rosalie rolled up her sleeves in an attempt to right a wrong, the newspaper reporters would invariably point out that she was just another wealthy suburban girl who might talk a good game but who still went home every night to a warm and sumptuous bed.

And if Rosalie's family's good fortune wasn't enough to live down, there was always the issue of her mother, Mary, and her sister, Louise — both proud members of the New York Anti-Suffrage Association (which officially represented *the one thing* that Rosalie was most opposed to).[4] Her mother, in particular, had a reputation for belligerence, and had hated the idea of Rosalie's campaigning for the votes-for-women cause earlier that summer. Rosalie feared her mother, who came from one of the oldest, most aristocratic families on Long Island,[5] would completely disown her if she followed through on the daring plan now forming in her mind. Her mother's people were conservative through and through, so much so that her mother claimed they had actually supported King George rather than the Colonies in the American Revolution. The Joneses of Long Island were accustomed to associating with those already in power rather than those who merely sought to obtain it.

And there were other obstacles that would need overcoming as well, including Rosalie's previous anxieties about public speaking. In her first attempt, years earlier, she had had to fight back nervousness and self-doubt just to speak to three people and a dog! Still, with practice she'd gotten better, so much so that the previous year she had delivered a fiery women's rights speech with well-known suffragists Harriet Stanton Blatch and Alva Belmont right on the corner of Wall Street. The crowd had thrown tomatoes and eggs in her direction but Rosalie had found her voice, and she wasn't about to surrender it to a bunch of angry, fearful men.[6]

The boldness of Rosalie's latest idea frightened her a bit, but it was still less intimidating than those early speaking engagements, which had caused her knees to wobble and her voice to quiver. It was true that neither Rosalie nor Ida had all the answers about their latest proposed adventure — in fact, they still had plenty of questions — but they agreed to meet the very next day, at the suffrage headquarters in New York City, to see if others liked the idea as much as they did.

It was a Monday, and before noon had arrived they had put up signs at headquarters asking for volunteers — and, as luck would have it, they already had their first: Lavinia Dock.[7]

Rosalie and Ida could hardly believe their good fortune. Lavinia was some twenty-five years older than Rosalie and had done practically everything there was to do in life. She had graduated from the first nursing school in America, served as a superintendent at Bellevue Hospital in New York and at Johns Hopkins School for Nursing, authored several respected books on her profession, delivered lectures at the famous Chicago World's Fair, and cared for the poor at the Henry Street Settlement in New York City.[8] And now she had pledged herself to march alongside Rosalie and Ida as the army's "Surgeon General."

Rosalie, Ida, and Lavinia worked together that afternoon to fill in the details of the march they would soon need to share with the newspapers and magazines.

The start date was set for December 16 — an ideal time so far as Rosalie was concerned. First, it was near enough to the holidays that the people they would encounter on their march would be truly local rather than well-to-do summer tourists. Second, it would ensure that their cause received maximum news coverage. Newspapers and magazines were often short of meaningful news stories around the holidays, and here was an issue of true and timely importance. Finally, Christmastime — ripe for miracles of all sorts — would set an ideal tone for their unlikely journey, and at a time when everyday citizens were uniquely inclined to feel sympathy toward those facing hardship or deprivation.

Every pilgrimage needed a worthy terminus, however, and as Rosalie, Ida, and Lavinia puzzled over the possibilities that afternoon in New York City they saw that theirs, too, required a grand destination. Rosalie suggested Albany, New York, as a worthy goal — it was, after all, the capital city of the state thought to be the most influential in America, and thus a place where life-changing laws and policies were made. Pilgrims often marched toward the kind of cities where men of great power and learning issued decrees. Now that American women had found a cause whose spirit was worth walking for, why shouldn't they choose a destination equally meaningful? Militant suffragettes living half a world away had recently completed a votes-for-women pilgrimage from Edinburgh to London, and yet it had taken them nearly five weeks to cover a distance that Rosalie planned to cover in half that time.[9] America had never seen a march for equal rights anything like the length and scope of the ambitious hike Rosalie planned on conducting.

It was decided: Albany was to be the destination, and if Rosalie and her suffragettes could time their march just right, they would arrive in time for the swearing-in of the new Governor on January 1, 1913. Governor-elect William Sulzer appeared as if he might be sympathetic to their cause, though it was often difficult to tell with male politicians. The more progressive among them talked a good game, but when the chips were down, they often sighed, threw up their hands, and said something to the effect of, "I tried, ladies, I really did. But the resistance was just too fierce. Better luck next year."

Governor-elect Sulzer was thought to be a supporter of the cause, but he, too, had waffled just a month prior, on the occasion of a torch-lit suffrage parade in New York City. Before the election Mr. Sulzer had seemed primed to participate. He had even telegrammed the Men's League for Equal Suffrage, saying: "Will be glad to join the parade. I take deep interest in the cause."[10] But on the eve of the march he had, predictably, reversed himself, telling a reporter from the *New York Times*, "I cannot take part in the parade. I shall be out of town." Rosalie had taken part in the votes-for-women parade, and it had convinced her more than ever that momentum was swinging in the direction of the suffragettes, if only they could take the movement from the streets to the seats of power in Albany.

So with Ida and Lavinia at her side, Rosalie determined she and her fellow suffrage pilgrims wouldn't just hike hundreds of wintry miles to wave votes-for-women signs at the Governor's inauguration; they would also hand-deliver their votes-for-women message to the Governor. It would only be fitting for this promising, if unproven, governor to greet General Rosalie Jones and her troops in person, especially after they had sojourned so far to see him.

Finally, the pilgrims had to determine how best to get their message out to the many passersby and onlookers they were sure to encounter. They decided, in the true spirit of a democratic march, that each suffrage pilgrim would be provisioned with a knapsack (yellow, for the color of the cause), to be filled with leaflets, buttons, pamphlets, and other educational literature. The marchers would also wear suffrage sashes with the words "Votes for Women" printed on them.

Rosalie's proposed march already numbered three core members — Rosalie, Lavinia, Ida. Several dozen more at suffrage headquarters talked excitedly about perhaps joining up. Still it would be necessary for more enlistees and recruits to join along Rosalie's proposed route if they were to make it all the way to the capital.

Rosalie and Ida had less than a week to finalize their plans if they wanted to stick to their schedule. Rosalie would be out of town until Thursday, but she would continue to plan and to strategize while she was away, she promised. In the meantime Ida, Lavinia, and the rest of suffrage headquarters would continue working on the details of the march. Perhaps most importantly, they would begin leaking word of their proposed adventure to New York City's famously skeptical press.

✧   ✧   ✧

When Rosalie opened the door to headquarters a few days later, she found herself surrounded by reporters and swamped by questions. Would she or would she not be commanding the "march" to Albany? Already rumors were flying that the General had reconsidered the harrowing journey while she had been away.[11]

Rosalie met the doubters with a cheerful smile. Of course she would still be leading the march. Yes, "Colonel" Ida Craft would still be her second-in-command. And not only were the two of them still marching, they were, upon further reflection, duly resolved to stick with the march from beginning to end, even through Christmas.

Any other questions?

The reporters demanded all the details, and Rosalie did her best to answer them point for point. About lodging, she patiently explained that the marchers hoped to stay in hotels and inns located along the route. Friends and supporters could then contact them by letter at the towns on their scheduled route in care of "Votes-for-Women Pilgrimage." The most vital details, she assured them, would be arranged for as she mustered her army in the coming days.

What's more, there was a new addition to the plan — one that made the General swell with pride. She would be entrusted to carry to the Governor-elect a confidential message signed by the presidents of all the important New York suffrage associations. Rosalie herself had written and decorated the suffrage scroll in a manner meant to evoke the illuminated manuscripts of the Middle Ages.[12] The latest plans called for the signed and sealed parchment to be carried along the pilgrims' route almost like an Olympic torch.[13]

A supply "wagon" had been arranged for, too, which would follow the pilgrims with an abundance of buttons, badges, circulars, and leaflets, as well as food, if Ida had anything to say about it. Now that Rosalie had become widely known as "General" of the impending march on the capital, it only made sense, following the military analogy, that Ida be declared "Colonel." In addition to being Rosalie's second-in-command, Ida had declared herself, somewhat comically, to be the head of the Commissary Department — in charge of food for the trip, though she wouldn't yet say exactly what she had planned for the menu.[14]

"Perhaps the pilgrims themselves will need a lift," someone said, apropos of the news of this supply car.

"Perhaps they will," Colonel Craft replied, and Rosalie couldn't be blamed if she winced a bit at her comrade's hasty reply, which made it sound as if the suffragettes would be accepting rides. Ida was so energetic, so eager to rush into the fray, that she could sometimes speak a bit carelessly. Rosalie was a more measured speaker than her over-exuberant yet loyal friend, but that was perhaps to the good; there was little sense in a general and her colonel having exactly the same aptitudes.

"What will you do if it snows?" one of the older, more practical suffragists asked, a look of concern painted across her face.

Before the General could open her mouth to reply, a friend of the cause answered, "Their hearts are so warm they will melt the snow." Rosalie couldn't have said it better herself.

Someone else wanted to know what on earth they would do in the hours when they weren't hiking. Rosalie patiently explained that they would be making appearances at dinners, banquets, dances, and teas. They'd visit factories and schools, too. They'd go anywhere they were welcome to share their passionate speeches.

Rosalie marveled at the growing list of women who had pledged to walk with them when they marched out of the city on Monday morning. One, Velma Swanstrom Howard, had even volunteered to lend Swedish snowshoes to pilgrims in need.

Would Velma be there bright and early at 9:15 a.m. on Monday, then?

"I surely will," Velma replied, "if the Lord is willing, and I wake up."

Rosalie smiled and reassured the would-be hikers that she had noticed a growing excitement about the suffrage hike in her recent travels around the state. "They have read about it in the New York papers," she said, "and I overheard conversations on the trains. Sometimes when I was writing in a hotel I heard…. 'The pilgrims are going to pass through here on their way to Albany!'"

It was lovely now to be among friends and supporters at suffrage headquarters, and exciting to think about all the people who would be joining their cause. Still, Rosalie knew that for all the preliminary positive coverage her idea for a suffrage hike had received, the city's newspapers bristled with reactionary voices speaking out in opposition to the march. One man had been quoted in the *Times* saying that Rosalie's "sensational hike" would cost suffragists 100,000 votes in the next election.[15]

But General Jones did what she could to push these negative thoughts aside and focus on what needed to be accomplished before Sunday, December 15 — the day before the march — at which time she and Ida would host a "preparation tea" for those prospects who might like to enlist in their votes-for-women army. Already there was talk that Rosalie's "march" would be militant in nature, like the recent marches of their sister suffragettes in Great Britain. Rosalie needed to think of a creative and convincing way to remind the anxious that their intentions were wholly peaceful.

✿   ✿   ✿

Sunday's "preparation tea" came slowly, then all at once.

Rosalie woke early, anxious at the day before her, and dressed in a silk gown appropriate for a tea-time gathering.[16] On the way out the door she put on her coat to be safe. After all, it was December in New York City, and there would no doubt be some chilly breezes blowing up Madison Avenue when she reached headquarters.

Plans had fallen into place nicely in the last several days. General Jones and the other "officers" in the suffragette army had agreed that a proper march ought to have drums, and they had subsequently begun looking for a woman drummer. Meanwhile, Olive Schultz had agreed to lead the procession, motoring out in front of Rosalie as they reached each town to let the villagers know the all-women army was coming in peace. Doves would be released to announce the approach of the pilgrims as they neared each new town in turn.

Mr. George Newman of the Men's League for Equal Suffrage arrived at the preparation tea all smiles, dressed quite nattily with a red carnation in his buttonhole. He promised that a sign would be placed on one of the two supply cars that would read: "Men, Vote for Women in 1915."

Another suffrage supporter, one Alphonse Major, was selected to serve in a support role for the expedition. Mr. Major would drive the support car the whole way, sticking to the pilgrims "as faithfully as cement" as one reporter put it. He would carry the soldiers' luggage, their signs and pamphlets, food, and plenty of raincoats for the snow and freezing rain expected on the way. He would also, said *Woman's Journal*, "slay any wolves" who emerged from the anti-suffrage strongholds along the route.[17]

Woman's Journal didn't mean *wolves* to be taken literally, of course; it simply meant that Alphonse would be on hand if troublemakers who didn't believe in a woman's right to vote threatened the march — and of these there were frighteningly many. None of the women of Rosalie's army wanted to deal with wolves at Christmastime, though they would if they must. They had already shown themselves capable of great sacrifice, for to make their hike they would be giving up holidays with loved ones. But that was okay, because among the foot soldiers who had pledged themselves to the journey they had discovered a new family of sisters who loved them well.

George Newman had in tow that day a handmade sign on white cloth with Olive's official title, "Scout Car," painted on it, and when he and Olive went outside to take pictures, they asked Rosalie to come along. The General was glad to oblige, though she had the good sense to put her winter coat on first.

The greatest surprise of the preparation tea wasn't George with his hand-painted signs and debonair dress, however. Instead, a volunteer named Elizabeth stole the show. Lo and behold, "Elizabeth" (whose letter of interest had, tellingly enough, *not* been accompanied by a picture) was revealed to be a dog — an African terrier to be exact. Her owner was a cigarette-smoking, alcohol-loving British suffragette named Inez Craven, whose reputation for violent protest had preceded her to the States and set Rosalie and her officers on edge. The journalists positively adored Mrs. Craven, if for no other reason than the outspoken Englishwoman provided great quotes and even better stories. Rosalie wasn't sure who was more attention-hungry: the dog or its owner?

Rosalie, Lavinia, and Ida learned from Mrs. Craven that Elizabeth had been born halfway across the world in Nairobi. Surely, if Elizabeth the Suffrage Dog could make it to New York City all the way from Kenya, she could make it to the capital! Elizabeth, Mrs. Craven informed them, would wear purple, green, and white ribbons on her collar — the colors of the British suffrage movement, since Kenya was a British protectorate. Indeed, Elizabeth had already wolfed down the celebratory layer cake offered at the preparation tea as if were her last supper!

The officers in Rosalie's army had likewise developed a fine and growing appetite for adventure. Colonel Craft — she the self-appointed head of the Commissary Department — had with her usual guile yesterday secured for Rosalie's army a perfect little trail mix, complete with raisins, chocolates, and peanuts. Surgeon General Dock, meanwhile, had acquired emergency supplies donated to the pilgrims by Lavinia's fellow nurses at the Henry Street Settlement. The outside of the medic's box — a delicate pasteboard wrapped with a yellow ribbon — was as dainty a thing as Rosalie could imagine, and yet atop it was a printed sign that read: "First-aid is all right for bruises, but nothing will save us but votes for all."

It was comforting to have Lavinia, an expert nurse, pledged to the march as surgeon general. Still, Rosalie couldn't help but wonder if it would be Lavinia, some twenty-five years her senior, who might end up needing the most nursing on the difficult journey to come.

The preparation tea had turned into something of a potluck. Someone had contributed cookies, and Rosalie had brought some jam to make tongue-in-cheek "anti-suffrage" jelly sandwiches — anti-suffrage because the jelly had been made on her mother's estate on Long Island. Her mother disapproved of Rosalie's actions, but what could she do? Rosalie was an adult now, and was free to make an adult's decisions — and suffer the consequences, too.

Most recently Mary Jones had taken the case against her daughter's activities directly to the press. "The idea is ridiculous…. I am going to do everything in my power to prevent my daughter from starting on the trip," her mother had told reporters, much to Rosalie's horror. Then, to make matters worse, Mary Jones had added, "She has made two other trips, and I could not restrain her…. She campaigned on Long Island for ten days last summer, and in the early fall made a month's tour of Ohio…. This was bad enough, but to think of a band of young women walking along the road to [the capital] is a great deal worse."[18]

To her army regulars Rosalie distributed walking sticks from the family's Long Island woods. The Alpine staffs could be used as walking sticks, as pointers to show the way, or even as weapons of self-defense, if the occasion ever arose. But mostly the General had commissioned them to mark the exceptional event that would begin the next day at 9:15 in the morning: the start of the greatest and longest women's rights march the country had ever known.

One side of Rosalie's own walking stick had the initials R. G. J., and the other side had the march's rallying cry: "Votes for Women." Rosalie presented her second-in-command with a similar staff. This one, easily six feet tall, towered over the diminutive, bespectacled Ida.

Along the route the pilgrims would place staves decorated with "Votes for Women" streamers, and a new notch would be cut into their walking sticks for every town they passed. In this way they would spread word of their cause like modern-day Paul Reveres.

Rosalie hoped the rank-and-file privates in her army would bring their own walking sticks, and by the look of the store-bought models in front of her now, many already had. Nearly three dozen brave women had said yes to Rosalie's earlier call for volunteers, and each was now given what the General called "light marching equipment," including sweaters, long skirts, and walking boots. Knapsacks filled with brochures and pamphlets were handed out to each pilgrim to be distributed to potential converts along the way. Peanuts, chocolate, and sandwiches were stashed here and there in backpacks as secret caches of sustenance.

"We could go to Albany by train, but the purpose of our propaganda is to reach the women of the country towns," Colonel Craft announced to all those assembled. "On our way to Albany we expect to be joined in our pilgrimage by members of the suffrage societies of the towns at which we stop."[19]

The preparation tea had been held at headquarters on Manhattan's Madison Avenue — not very far from the famous Madison Square Park and Central Park. Madison Avenue had become synonymous with buying and advertising, and with the holiday season in full swing the busy thoroughfare fairly buzzed with big spenders. The Garment District was also mere blocks away. There poor immigrant women slaved to produce the fashions worn by so many American women.

Fashion had changed a great deal since the Industrial Revolution, before which many women had made their own clothes for themselves and their families. But as the country had grown wealthier and more industrial and young women moved from the country to the city, it became more important than ever to dress for success. Many, if not most, busy women lacked the time to make their own clothes, so New York City, and the Garment District in particular, made their clothes for them.

So when Rosalie told her all-women corps that there would be charity dances and fundraisers and teas en route, the suffragette recruits suddenly grew very nervous. How on earth, they wondered, could they dress to be both marching soldiers and fashionable ladies? How could they impress those who might wish to donate time and money to the cause if they appeared before them in muddy boots — "kickers," as they were known.

Rosalie assured them that they could indeed dress the part of rough-and-ready soldiers of fortune on the march and yet dress fashionably enough to win the equal rights battles waged in drawing rooms, tea parlors, and dance floors. General Jones, for instance, had selected a creamy lace gown for today's tea, accessorized with a scarlet sash around the waist and a lace hat with a wreath of small rosebuds. It was in this "uniform" that she now addressed her would-be soldiers. "We must honor our entertainers and the suffrage societies of New York by looking our best," she said. [20] They would pack their evening gowns and dresses in advance, she told them, and ship them to arrive in the few towns along the way where such fineries would be needed.

Of course the more practical among the women pilgrims had already begun to talk about what they would wear while they were slogging through the mud. "For goodness' sake, grease your shoes well," one of the suffragettes cautioned, though she might just as well have skipped the warning. You didn't have to be an experienced hiker to know there was nothing worse than walking mile after mile in wet woolen socks when a remedy as simple as waxing one's shoes might do the trick.

One of the older prospective pilgrims chimed in next. "Best thing in the world for your feet is to soap them good before you pull on your socks," she said. This particular volunteer had come ready to march, carrying her staff and backpack to the planning meeting. Low-heeled boots, they agreed, would be the best footwear by far. Long skirts would be unavoidable; they were a de facto uniform for women at the time. Rosalie agreed with suffragists like Carrie Chapman Catt who had urged women to abandon their skirts for trousers. Less than ten days ago in New York City, in fact, Mrs. Catt had had told them, "Make a bonfire of your hats, throw away your corsets, and wear trousers instead of these ridiculous tight skirts."[21]

But one thing at a time. If General Rosalie Jones had to choose between winning either the Battle of the Pants or the War for Women's Votes, she would choose the latter. Jessie Hardy Stubbs, who was to be Rosalie's army's handpicked "War Correspondent," agreed wholeheartedly with the General's no-nonsense recommendations for marching uniforms. "I'm going to wear a little flannel shirt," Jessie announced, "a regular boy's shirt, and over that a sweater and then a lightweight walking dress."[22] Above all, Jessie warned, suffragettes should not trifle with fancy undergarments or slips — wool tights and low-heeled sturdy walking boots would serve them twice as well.

Rosalie interrupted the chatter, sensing that her troops might lose sight of their larger objective if they continued to debate outdoor fashions. "Do listen, everybody!" she shouted above the cacophony of voices. "We are to meet tomorrow morning at 9 o'clock at 242nd Street and Broadway. When we start we will lift the cry, 'Votes for Women' and we'll keep that up all the way to Albany — stopping to eat and sleep, of course. There's going to be a drummer at the start-off — a female drummer — she is to beat the signal."

Rosalie had taken great pains to ensure that, whenever possible, the women in the march would fill the roles typically reserved for men and boys. Why couldn't a woman beat on a drum or blow a horn just as well as a man?

Someone asked Colonel Craft by what method the hikers intended to reach their would-be converts.

"House-to-house canvass," Ida replied. "It's the only way to get in real touch with the women outside of New York City."

Ida was a marvel of energy and high spirit, and Rosalie knew that her good friend would never leave her side. Rosalie couldn't help but be impressed as she took a final look out at her soldiers — what fine examples of their sex, indeed of humanity itself, they appeared to her. They were a small but mighty group of women.

Still, for as well as the preparation tea had gone, many of those who had appeared in their best gowns for high tea and biscuits had demurred when asked to confirm their involvement in the march. Harriet May Mills, for example, had taken suddenly ill, and would not be fit for the beginning stages, though she promised to join the pilgrims as soon as she was able. Others made excuses when asked if they had purchased their walking sticks, saying they couldn't yet commit and would buy them at the last minute if they were able to make tomorrow's march.

Even among the "maybes" and "mights," a generous percentage of her volunteers would most likely get cold feet at the eleventh hour, Rosalie realized with a sigh. Still, she had some cause for optimism. At the very least, she could absolutely count on Ida, Lavinia, and Jessie to be there at the starting line. And besides, how many generals in all of human history could lay claim to going into battle with a solider named Elizabeth the Suffrage Dog?

CHAPTER 2:
FORWARD MARCH!

Now was no time to falter or lose faith, Rosalie reminded herself as she stared out on the crowd of nearly five hundred marchers, supporters, well-wishers, and onlookers that had assembled at the corner of Broadway and 242nd Street in the Bronx. Many of her fellow votes-for-women supporters had woken up early to ride the Broadway subway line to make it to the staging ground in time for the start of the women's march into history that was to commence today, Monday, December 16.

Colonel Craft read out the projected itinerary for a march that would take them north out of the city along the old Albany Postal Road that ran along the east bank of the Hudson River. If all went well, by that very evening Rosalie's army would be in Irvington; Tuesday they would overnight in Ossining; Wednesday in Peekskill; Thursday meant Fishkill; and Friday would be spent in Wappingers Falls — including a ball in their honor scheduled for that night. Saturday night would be spent in Poughkeepsie, and Sunday in a place called Rhinebeck. On Monday they hoped to pass through Red Hook so that by Tuesday evening, December 24th, they might reach Hudson and spend Christmas Eve and Day there before plunging ahead to the many small towns and villages that lay between Hudson and the capital city. Altogether they planned to march nearly two hundred miles, including detours, between now and New Year's Eve.

"This pilgrimage is only a starter," Ida declared,[1] her cheeks flushing with wintertime cold. "We will have others…. We could go to Albany by train, but the purpose… is to reach the women of the country." Ida further promised passionate speeches from the talented orators who had lately joined Rosalie's army — including most especially Jessie Hardy Stubbs.

The National Women's Party to which Jessie belonged was so proud of Jessie they had already declared her "a part of the history of the national suffrage movement," snapping a photograph of their star "lecturer" dressed in a suit and a cloche hat, her bright eyes burning like dark coals.[2] Jessie's wry, enigmatic smile seemed to say, "I see something you cannot yet see."

In her publicity photo Jessie wore a short-brimmed hat, a smart plaid suit with a sailor-style blouse, and a small fashionable purse tucked beneath her left elbow. Here was a woman who would not be slowed by excessive baggage or supposed burdens of her sex. "She is well-known and beloved throughout the country," the caption accompanying her photo read, "for her speaking and organizing ability and for her loyal service… [S]he was formerly National Press Chairman of the Congressional Union." Jessie was a Midwesterner based in Chicago, but she had strong ties to New York State, where her father, Major A. L. Hardy, had attended the Peekskill Military Academy. Jessie had risen to become one of the most prominent organizers in that state's Suffrage Association, despite having heard nothing from her father since she was eight years old. Major Hardy had split from Jessie and her mother, and had refused any relationship with them ever since.

Rosalie was thankful to have such a graceful and passionate spokeswoman as Jessie serving as the marchers' war correspondent and press agent. The General was also fortunate, she knew, to have the services of such an impassioned canvasser as Ida. But Rosalie was still the general, and it was up to her now to rally the nearly three dozen women who had signed up to tramp along with her, at least until the first stop at Yonkers.

Should Rosalie have waited until she had more foot soldiers enlisted and more detailed plans made? How many among her platoon would she lose after the first day? It was all well and good to show up at the starting line, but wouldn't much of this "moral support" evaporate when dinnertime arose and the hunger pangs started?

Rosalie checked the time: nearly quarter to ten! Second-guessing and self-doubts would have to wait for some other time. Already, they had fallen more than a half-hour behind schedule. The General grabbed her megaphone and strode to the front of the line. Yellow was the color of her cause, but Rosalie had been determined to wear a white hat; it felt right, and besides, it would help the other marchers identify her more easily.

"Marchers form in line!" Rosalie called above the din as her officers fell in behind her in rank and file: Colonel Craft came first, wearing a long brown and black coat comically overloaded with leaflets and circulars.[3] Behind Ida stood Rosalie's stalwart surgeon general Lavinia "Little Doc" Dock, and behind Lavinia marched Katherine Abbot, beating out a martial rhythm on her drums. Katherine's timing was perfect as she gave Rosalie's troops the boost they needed at exactly the moment they needed it. Next came Jessie, their war correspondent and walking public relations agent, wearing a white hat of her own and stepping exuberantly. Behind Jessie walked nearly three dozen "privates" in Rosalie's army who intended to hike at least to the first stop in Yonkers, including three — Alice L. Clark, Katherine Stiles, and Sybil Wilbur — who hoped to march most of the way alongside the army's "high command."

Alice was a well-conditioned hiker and a busy organizer. The prior year, while acting as the secretary of the League of Self-Supporting Women, Alice had compiled a complete catalogue detailing each and every legislator's views on votes for women and presented it to the state suffrage society as a kind of scouting report. To the extent that the male legislators in Albany could be said to be the enemy of women's equality, Alice believed in knowing the enemy in detail.

Katherine, on the other hand, claimed to be on the hike mostly for its health benefits. Katherine's husband, Meredith N. Stiles, wrote for the Associated Press, an organization whose reporters regarded journalistic objectivity with the same degree of reverence the suffrage pilgrims reserved for gender equality. Katherine was justifiably proud of her evolving identification with votes-for-women activism and yet, given her husband's position with the most important news service in the nation, her role in the pilgrimage would have to be underplayed to avoid raising eyebrows.

The "war correspondents" covering the march on the capital were expected to be windows to the real story — the historic march of Rosalie's army — not the story themselves, and sometimes this, too, seemed unfair. This was especially true for Sybil Wilbur, who, like Katherine, was an ardent suffragist who had pledged to travel nearly every step of the way with the pilgrims but didn't fully "count" as a hiker in the eyes of many of her coworkers in the press. Sibyl, covering the hike for the *American*, was all but forced to choose between her identity as an objective author-journalist (she had written the definitive biography of Christian Science founder Mary Baker Eddy) and as a trooper in Rosalie's army.

Still, regardless of their secret, or not-so-secret, beliefs, the men and women of the press corps had answered the bell and now stood ready to vote with their feet for an active interest, at the very least, in the cause of women's suffrage. Including reporters, about two hundred supporters, representing seven different organizations working to secure votes for women, now stood awaiting the signal. With a flourish Katherine Abbot beat on her snare drum, and the pilgrims felt the primal marching rhythm coursing through them.

Once the hubbub died down and her ranks closed in behind her, Rosalie called out "Forward!" and the marchers were off to the clicking of cameras trained on the platoon of proud women. Beside the long column of marchers were the police, on hand for crowd control, mounted on their well-groomed horses, the clip-clop of their hooves a percussive accompaniment to the pilgrims' own drummer girl.

Colonel Craft was positively giddy with excitement, darting in and out of the crowd of onlookers and curiosity-seekers distributing her pro-suffrage literature by the handful. "Remember that the age for slavery for women is past!" she exclaimed to one citizen after another.

Impulsively, Ida passed her circular to a heavy-set gentleman wearing a severe frown on his face. Much to her and everyone else's surprise, the stout man brightened, bowed, and said, "Thank you. You have my vote."

General Rosalie Jones thrilled as her troopers once more raised their battle cry: "Votes for women! Votes for women!"

Still, not everyone was so thrilled. Some jeered at Rosalie's army as it passed, telling them to go back home where they belonged. Their shrill, judgmental voices reminded Rosalie and Ida that their march would meet with much resistance once the pomp and circumstance of this opening parade had faded away. There would be many miles between towns and villages where they would be utterly without police protection, eerily quiet places along rural routes where dissenting voices would be amplified for miles rather than be drowned out by crowds of well-wishers.

The day had blessed them with perfect marching weather — crisp and calm and not too cold — and Rosalie noted with satisfaction that she and her army had already marched nearly a half-mile toward Yonkers, their intended lunchtime stop. General Jones was startled from her calculations by the sound of a door being opened. A woman emerged onto the porch of her simple frame house. She wore a pro-suffrage banner around her waist, and as the General and her army looked on she waved it above her head with such vigor that it caught on an overhanging tree branch. "Hurrah!" she shouted. "And good luck. I am with you!"

This same woman cheered them on until the very last of the march-ers strode past her — now with a newfound vigor.

They were approaching New York's city limits, and here their gentle-manly police escort bowed stiffly, and ushered the woman's army into the unknown. It was 10:15 a.m.

"Halt!" Rosalie shouted, surprised by how quickly the column of marching women stopped at her command. "Three Cheers!"

The suffragettes echoed her cheer, and the General ordered them forward once again. As they crossed from New York City into Yon-kers, Rosalie saw that the Yonkers police sergeant and a patrolman had taken up the peacekeeping baton and were prepared to escort the army into their fair city. A few moments later she noticed that Katherine's drumbeat had ceased — and very abruptly. Apparently, Katherine had thumped her drum so hard it had broken! Alphonse, the supply-car driver, eased his automobile up to the front, and stowed the broken instrument in the car.

Rosalie's army had its first casualty!

Was it possible to be overexcited at the prospect of votes for women? If the drum was any indication, Rosalie feared the answer might be *yes*.

The suffragette army now passed under the windows of a neighbor-hood trade school, and the students there opened up the windows to shout their support. The marchers were now an hour ahead of schedule. Thanks to Olive in the scout car motoring ahead to announce their coming, the local suffragists who were to provide that day's lunch had prematurely left their catering posts to hurry down to the town square, creating a sudden congestion.

The clock read 11:00 a.m. by the time they arrived in Getty Square at the very center of Yonkers. Already, the heart of the city had become a beehive of activity; it seemed as if half of the village's population had descended on the public square to witness history in the making.

Alphonse stopped the baggage car on the east side of the square, and the police chief, Daniel Wolff, made his way though the crowd wearing a "Votes for Women" badge in his buttonhole. "Ladies," the chief called out, "the permit has not arrived. There must be a delay." The announcement was met by groans of disappointment and boos.

How Rosalie hated permits! Since when did revolutions require permits? Had Washington required a permit to cross the Delaware? Had the patriots in Boston politely requested permission from city authorities to host their tea party? Societal transformation was achieved through action, not paperwork.

Why must achieving change in society be so difficult? Why must it require so many measured steps and fraught prior approvals? Hadn't the people back at suffrage headquarters in Manhattan handled these small details in advance so that she could focus on leadership? Rosalie hadn't exactly asked for a lesson on patience and humility, but perhaps she was getting one. Apparently, generals must be prepared to do a bit of everything, whether that meant making a speech, booking a room, or repairing the sole of a tired and worn-out shoe.

The police chief's special officer, Edward Welsh, was less apologetic about the army's problematic entrance into the city. He was complaining to one of the marchers that he and the chief had been on the verge of catching a pickpocket when Rosalie's army had stormed the square a full hour ahead of schedule. The officer was clearly bitter.

It turned out that the local suffragist who had originally requested the permit had not yet shown up at the square, and Chief Wolff could only suggest, politely but firmly, that a second application be taken out back at police headquarters; no meetings would be held until that time.

Worse, word now reached the General that Olive Schultz's scout car had since broken down and needed repairs.

Rosalie took quick inventory of the bad omens that she and her regular officers — Ida and Lavinia — had thus far been presented with. They were, in no particular order:

1. A broken car
2. A missing permit
3. A busted drum
4. A very miffed Special Officer Ed Welsh

And now she had word that George — George, the representative of the Men's League for Equal Suffrage; George with his delightful whiskers and cheerful demeanor who had accompanied Olive in the lead car — had disappeared. He had cited, among other obstacles big and small, his dog's absolute objection to Inez Craven's terrier, Elizabeth. More than likely the good man and his animal companion had simply had enough for the day, tucked tail, and gone back to the more knowable confines of New York City.

It was just then that the mayor arrived on the scene, bowing ostentatiously. The town's executive seemed intent on genuflecting repeatedly until Police Chief Wolff gave the politician a nudge — at which point he mounted the podium to say to Rosalie, "I welcome you to this city."

The mayor smiled beamishly at the resultant cheers, and repeated, "The city welcomes you!"

Once the crowd had quieted, the mayor went on to say that it was a real shame that these newly arrived pilgrims could not vote. The hikers thanked him heartily for his sentiments, still — why was it that politicians so seldom followed through on their promises once the speechmaking and glad-handing were over?

Rosalie was standing behind the mayor, and when one man looked at her especially intently and remarked, "*You* deserve to vote," she couldn't help but blush. Even women reporters often referred to her as "the young and pretty" Rosalie Jones in their columns, but Rosalie felt they should know better. It wasn't a woman's youthful good looks that made her a formidable suffragette but her passion for the cause and her determination to put the movement's principles into action. Had the same journalists gushed over the "the dashingly handsome" President Theodore Roosevelt? Of course not! They had simply referred to him by the titles he had rightly earned, such as *Colonel Roosevelt* or *Mr. President.*

Like many generals before and since, Rosalie was often more comfortable letting her actions speak for her, unlike Jessie Hardy Stubbs, whose words seemed to take on a life of their own when she was speechifying. Still, Rosalie was slowly learning to command her language in the same manner that she commanded her column of suffragettes. By the end of their long hike, she sincerely hoped she would have learned to command a crowd, like Jessie, with her words alone.

"Such a good city," Rosalie now said, simply and genuinely, to Yonkers' exuberant mayor. She ordered her army forward again, down Broadway to the headquarters of the Yonkers Woman Suffrage Association, which had arranged a more quiet sort of tea party welcome for the pilgrims.

Rosalie was enjoying a steaming cup, letting it warm her from within, when a messenger arrived with a kind note of support from Mr. Smith, a Yonkers city official, who compared this march to that of the Boston Tea Party itself. The issues, Mr. Smith wrote in his note, were exactly the same: taxation without representation. The women of New York — and nearly every other state in the freest nation on earth — could be taxed without having so much as a vote in which politicians represented them.

Well, tea was not only a cause worth rebelling for but a heartening gift after nearly four hours spent in the cold out-of-doors. Still, the dozens of news reporters covering the Yonkers stop appeared to look down their noses at the simple soup given Rosalie's army with their tea. The General couldn't help but notice that a group of them disappeared toward the end of the luncheon, no doubt to find finer cuisine or an obliging tavern at which to whet their whistle.

By 1:00 p.m. Rosalie gave the call to march again, and with a little encouragement her officers and privates were up on their feet, hiking out of Yonkers. They were not alone. Police on horseback rode in support, and the police chief himself traveled alongside in his patrol car. Some spirited soul had decked out the two city cars in yellow streamers, and the special effect lent both pomp and pep to the afternoon's proceedings. And there was Colonel Craft again, running about with her circulars, darting madly into the crowds to explain all the benefits women could expect once they received the vote. Rosalie marveled at her colonel's courage — a different kind of courage than her own, but courage nevertheless.

A half-mile outside of Yonkers a group of men, dirty from work, watched Rosalie's army approach. They seemed to wear the kinds of grins men usually reserved for things they found mildly threatening.

And what did Ida do? Ida met their gaze directly, and took off running toward them, extending her leaflets in their direction as she ran.

"Look who's coming!" one of the men hollered to his compatriots, who seemed no longer amused but genuinely startled. The first man succeeded in getting away from her, but Colonel Craft proved much too fast for those remaining. Ida gave each of the workers a smile and a suffrage pamphlet and sent them on their way.

Even though they had now passed the Yonkers city limits, Police Chief Wolff, his patrol car crammed full of newspaper reporters, decided to continue his personal escort a little while longer. Apparently, the reporters inside were having a heated debate as to whether suffragettes had the right to practice civil disobedience — breaking laws for their cause. Rosalie's army had not broken any laws thus far on their journey at that point, but who could tell what lay in store.

Shortly after 2:00 p.m. Rosalie afforded her troops a brief stop again at a small roadside inn a few miles beyond the city limits. She was trying to acclimate her conscripts gradually. A number had already said their thanks and taken their quiet leave back in Yonkers; thankfully, however, several new marchers had joined up there as well, including a local reverend. Apparently, even God thought it just that women should have the vote, at least in Reverend Tambly's eyes.

At the inn Rosalie dropped gratefully into a rocking chair for a brief instant and watched as everyone took tea and coffee together. The army privates nibbled on the chocolate that Colonel Craft had wisely brought along. Rosalie, cheered by the sight of the sweetly fatigued conviviality around her, asked aloud if anyone in the room could sing. A half dozen women said they could, but alas they had left their sheet music at home. Sheet music was not a requirement, the General assured them. What soldiers lacked in technical perfection they made up for in spirit!

At Rosalie's urging one of the journalists leapt to the piano, and an older woman draped in streamers began an improvised dance that looked something like a cross between the Double Shuffle and the Turkey Trot! She quit just as suddenly as she had started, as if she had surprised herself with her exuberance, and made way for a couple of the reporters.

Unfortunately there was little time for dancing, and just twenty minutes after arriving at the inn, the General enjoined her corps to begin the march again. Police Chief Wolff reluctantly took his leave, too, as did many from the Yonkers contingent who had walked several more miles beyond town than intended, caught up in the sprit of the day and the righteousness of the cause.

The afternoon took the marchers through some of the most beautiful countryside north of New York City — impressively wooded hills, with the ever-present Hudson River flowing near to the side of the road as they marched. Glancing now and then behind her, Rosalie observed that most of the day-hikers had gone now, and it was left to the determined handful to grit their teeth and continue on.

Rosalie led her remaining troops into Irvington-on-the-Hudson just as darkness began to paint the Hudson Valley sky with its somber tones. At times it had seemed that there were more newspaper reporters following Rosalie's band of pilgrims than actual marchers, and whereas journalists were often short on action they certainly never lacked for opinions. The General had just now led her army to the outskirts of Irvington-on-the-Hudson, their first night's stop, and yet the reporters had already begun to churn out headlines from the suffrage hike's first day — which had, admittedly, been a mixed bag.

Jessie had been wonderful in rallying the Yonkers faithful, but many of the fair-weather supporters from the city had left off there, and the privates who remained had struggled with the physical challenge of the road. The stop in Yonkers and at the inn outside the city had taken up more time, too, than either Rosalie or Colonel Craft had planned, and as they marched into Irvington now, a night chill descended on the Hudson River town. The street up which they hiked, Broadway, was known as Millionaire's Row for the many mansions and estates that lined the road, and the sight of these gentrified homes presented to the General a strange contrast to the humble condition of her once-spirited female corps.

"We are now down to brass tacks," said Rosalie when, footsore and weary, she turned to face her troops.

The handful of war correspondents following the pilgrims could be a hard-hearted bunch, and where Rosalie characteristically saw hope, the journalists typically saw confusion and despair. By Jessie's count, ten reporters — representing what she called the most powerful newspapers and journals in New York — had agreed to follow the march all, or most, of the way to the capital. Many other newsmen and women would come and go, reporting from the front as the army marched into their particular town or village. Still more would report from afar, re-writing or simply reprinting news of the hike as it came across the wire. While many of the correspondents covering the pilgrimage to Albany were known suffrage supporters, the objectivity of their profession demanded they represent their readers' questions and attitudes as much or more than their own. Indeed, much of their coverage appeared without so much as a byline.

Similarly, Katherine Stiles of Brooklyn was proud of her identity as a New York suffragist and yet, given her husband's position with the Associated Press, covering the march meant that her stalwart loyalty to the cause could also not be written about without casting wider doubts. Still, Rosalie and her officers honored Sibyl's and Katherine's dedication by assigning them honorary titles — "Corporal" for Katherine and "Private" for Sibyl.

Not all of the war correspondents following Rosalie and company were similarly inclined to support women's suffrage. Indeed, one reporter's bah-humbug dispatch from that day noted how many of the "friends" of the marchers had left for home after lunch in Yonkers. One mentioned that Rosalie's new friend and votes-for-women sympathizer, Police Chief Wolff, had taken many of the dropouts home in a paddy wagon that he had arranged for in advance. Mr. Wolff was a very shrewd and practical lawman and he understood that a great majority of well-intentioned people would find cause to drop out of any great venture when they realized the sacrifice it required. These supporters preferred hot baths and clean linens to a walking stick and a sign. Some activists were adventurers — true expeditionaries — while others were destined to support the cause from desks and drawing rooms; to distinguish between them, reporters often ascribed the label *suffragette* to the former, *suffragist* to the latter

Why couldn't the gaggle of naysaying reporters be more supportive? They seemed to derive pleasure from failure. Here was one story, for example, that after referring to Rosalie's troops as "valiant women" went on to describe their entry into Irvington thusly: "The pomp and circumstance that marked their departure from New York were gone; the flags had unfurled; the drum, which was to have cheered lagging footsteps, was broken and the drummer departed." Others reported that even Elizabeth the Suffrage Dog and her owner, Inez Craven, had quit in Yonkers, claiming that the spirited animal that was to have been the mascot for the march had been too tuckered out to put one paw in front of the other.

What was it about the mostly male reporters that seemed always to want to find a chink in a woman's armor, ever ready to summon details that made the leaders of the cause itself seem less than what they had first appeared? One reporter even relished the irony of the General's stepping into the pilot car briefly as her army had marched out of Manhattan earlier that morning, as if that brief moment somehow revealed Rosalie's secret desire to ride rather than to walk. In fact, Rosalie had committed to tramping every mile of the journey, and she was determined to keep that promise.

Thus when the General spoke with the reporters upon reaching Irvington, she couldn't help but needle them a bit in reaction to their first-day negativity. Women, she told them, would one day go to war, make laws for the nation, and put a stop to the rampant voter fraud and ballot-fixing that had become the norm at Tammany Hall.

It comforted Rosalie to make a mental list of all that had gone right on this first day. First, they had left New York unmolested, without angry men blocking their path or screaming obscenities at them, as had happened elsewhere in the world where suffragettes had dared demonstrate in the streets. And they had made it to Irvington before nightfall. Along the way there had been many other pleasures to savor. Earlier that very morning, as they had readied themselves to march, a fancy touring car had pulled up behind them as they assembled in the streets. Rosalie's troops had gazed in the window to see that it was John D. Rockefeller, America's richest man by many accounts. At the time he had been frowning disapprovingly at what he no doubt saw as a gaggle of angry women blocking his path.

Rosalie was glad her female soldiers had had the good sense to let the industrialist pass, and equally pleased that they had not let the oil tycoon motor away completely without comment. "We'll stop at Tarrytown to see you!" the suffragettes had called after him, delighting in the deepening of his frown.[4]

Tarrytown was just a few miles away from Irvington, and was richer still than Millionaire's Row. Rockefeller had built his mansion, Kykuit, there seven years earlier, a six-storied, forty-room behemoth in gray stone whose showy extravagance had upset some in the working class.[5] America, it seemed, had devolved into haves and have-nots, and nowhere was that fact more evident than here, where not only Rockefeller but John Archbold, the president of Standard Oil, had built their mansions in a place that had stood for the freedom and dignity of the displaced and dispossessed seeking refuge on the Underground Railroad. Still, such men had been generous philanthropists of many worthwhile causes, showing that it was possible to have a kind heart even if it wasn't always for suffrage.

Well, Rosalie's army wouldn't be knocking on John D. Rockefeller's door — that was exactly the kind of negative publicity the General didn't want — but the thought was amusing and proved, if nothing else, that her army possessed yet another line of defense if needed: its wit.

The suffrage pilgrims were now many miles away from the Garment District near to where General Jones had first briefed her would-be troopers at the preparation tea; in fact, this very evening on their way into Irvington the army had passed the sandstone mile markers Benjamin Franklin had erected during his time as postmaster in the village. They had passed mile marker 27 on what locals had aptly named the Albany Post Road, for it had been designated over two hundred years before to carry mail between New York City and Albany. Mile marker 27 was an impressive feat for a first day's march, though it was true they had begun on the far north side of the city and had covered considerably less ground on their first day than Franklin's mileposts indicated.

Rosalie could also be grateful, at the end of this first day, for her marchers' safety. Her mother had warned her not to undertake this journey, not only because her mother was an Anti, but also because, like any good mother, she feared for her daughter's safety. The world seemed to grow more unsettled by the day. In Europe anarchists threatened the peace, and in places like Irvington and Tarrytown, New York, homegrown anarchists looked with increasing revulsion at the gaudy homes of the rich. Milwaukee was even more restive. Three months earlier, in October, an émigré from Bavaria, John Flammang Schrank, had reported that the ghost of assassinated president William McKinley appeared before him in a dream, asking that McKinley's death be avenged. The ghost had then pointed to a picture of Theodore Roosevelt.[6]

Schrank was a New Yorker and had traveled all the way to Milwaukee, via New Orleans, to try to kill the Progressive Party's nominee. Teddy Roosevelt had been one of the most vocal supporters of women's suffrage, and if an insane man could seek to kill a prominent leader because of his beliefs, no one in the public eye could be considered safe.

Thankfully, Colonel Roosevelt had recovered from the bullet lodged in his lung and had just the previous week attended the luncheon for the women of the National Progressive Conference in Chicago. Roosevelt had devoted his speech that day to the necessity of votes for women and had pointed out the awful irony that two of the most important voices in Progressive politics in the election that had recently concluded, Jane Addams and Frances Kellor, had been prevented from casting their vote in their respective states.[7]

The news elsewhere on that first night seemed equally troubling to the march and its prospects. In the national elections in November, votes for women had been narrowly defeated in Michigan, and now came charges of ballot-tampering and rigged voting contrived to deal the suffragist cause a loss.[8] The debate over the viability of those ballots was now in the hands of the courts, and the debacle in Michigan proved, if nothing else, that some would stop at nothing short of cheating to prevent the nation's women from exercising their civic right.

Thankfully, faithful supporters like Emily Ford Skeel — the suffrage pilgrims' host for the night — would never abandon them or their cause, no matter how many defeats they suffered. How many remarkable women — Mrs. Skeel was an author herself and the great-granddaughter of the creator of the first truly American dictionary, Noah Webster — had offered such acts of remarkable hospitality?[9] Not only had Emily Skeel offered Rosalie's army lodging for the night, but just now, after feeding them the most amazing dinner, Emily claimed she had another surprise in store for the weary pilgrims: foot doctors who had traveled all the way from New York City to treat the ailing feet of the suffering suffragettes![10]

Mrs. Skeel looked on expectantly as Rosalie debated. What to do with such a truly generous gift? In all of American history Rosalie could not recall a single instance in which a team of podiatrists had been imported to give foot massages to soldiers. Perhaps they ought to have been, but still: General Jones did not desire any special treatment. If men could march with aching feet on endlessly uncertain roads, her soldiers could, too. With sincerest regrets and effusive thanks to their hostess, Rosalie declined the foot treatment, and, she was pleased to note, so did Ida, Lavinia, and Jessie. The General and her officers thanked Emily once more for her incomparable hosting and excused themselves for the evening. Never, in their whole lives, had they been so thoroughly tired.

There were many real dangers yet to be faced by the votes-for-women pilgrims on their expedition, but Rosalie was too tired at the moment to consider them much further. Tomorrow evening Rosalie's army would, she hoped, reach Ossining, and Peekskill the night after that. If they could only keep their feet moving, they would reach Hudson by Christmas Eve and there find the warmth, merriment, and good cheer they needed to press on to the capital with their suffrage message for the new Governor for his inauguration on New Year's Day.

Along the way they planned to assure everyone they met that granting votes to women would not send the country into a tailspin, nor wreck peaceful and prosperous homes, nor disadvantage children, nor turn women into men, nor any of the other ugly bugaboos the Antis claimed.

Instead, votes for women promised to make the nation fairer and more just, extending to them the civil right American men had enjoyed almost since the time the revolutionary Benjamin Franklin had walked these streets as postmaster.

CHAPTER 3:
PILGRIMS FOUR

How hard it was to wake up early in the morning after a long day's hike! Yesterday Rosalie's army had been fueled by high hopes and good cheer, but on this second day everyone awoke footsore and groaning. Had someone been blowing reveille, the pilgrims might have rolled out of bed more eagerly. As things stood, it was left to General Jones to remind her platoon that there would be a roll call later that morning at St. Mark's Episcopal Church. With that, the weary suffragettes rolled out of bed, slung their knapsacks over their shoulders, and moved out.

Though the day had dawned sunny, the troopers now hiked into a wind so brisk it caught their yellow pennants and stretched them stiff. They had been on the march for no more than a few minutes when Ida, fresh from the night's sleep and full of energy, declared excitedly, "Let's call upon Miss Gould and distribute some of our literature!"[1]

The "Miss Gould" in question was none other than the heiress Helen Gould, whose estate, like so many of America's most wealthy citizens', was located hard on the Hudson River. Helen Gould was a young lady who, along with her sister, stood to inherit the riches of her father, Jay Gould, one of the ten richest men in America. How like Ida to suggest they wake up the heiress, unannounced, by knocking at her door. *Good morning, Miss Gould! Coffee this fine morning? Orange juice? No? Well, how about a votes-for-women brochure to chew on then?*

The General rejected the idea for the same reason she had resisted barnstorming John D. Rockefeller's home in Tarrytown. She suspected Miss Gould, in her heart of hearts, could relate to the pilgrims; like Rosalie, she came from New York, and like Rosalie, she had attended college in that city. Indeed, Miss Gould had been a "miss" now for nearly forty-five years. Surely she could comprehend life without a husband, and yet Helen Gould had recently shocked friends and family by announcing her engagement to a Mr. Finley J. Shephard of St. Louis. The headlines relayed the story of a woman who had dared to be choosy

"Colonel" Ida Craft

in her men, reading: "Eldest Daughter of Late Jay Gould Famed Over World for Gifts to Poor; Refused Many Former Proposals." Miss Gould, the article went on to note, was "one of the world's richest women."[2]

Rosalie surveyed her army, whose members met her gaze with good-natured mischief playing in their eyes. How badly they wanted to serve as Miss Gould's wake-up alarm! The reporters, too, enthusiastically embraced Ida's celebrity-chasing plan, and it wasn't hard to see why. Journalists loved a good, saucy celebrity story. "Miss Gould has succumbed to Cupid," Rosalie said to Ida, explaining her decision to take the high road. "We are vowed to suffrage."

The General was tempted, very tempted indeed, to plead the votes-for-women case to Helen Gould, but she resisted the pressure and stuck to her private sense of what was right. After all, the pilgrims had a mission, and they certainly didn't need the extra sensationalism or ill will sure to be created by unannounced visits to America's most high-profile citizens. Rosalie did agree, though, to cut across the expansive lawns of Miss Gould's estate in order to shorten the suffragettes' journey, and this seemed to at least somewhat appease Ida and the journalists.

"Right turn!" Rosalie commanded to Colonel Craft's delight, as the pilgrims set off across the expansive grounds owned by the icon known as "the best beloved woman in America."[3] Still, for the moment, all the laurels belonged to Rosalie, for her troops had just voted her "the greatest commander in chief" for choosing such an expeditious shortcut.

But optimism soon gave way to disappointment when they found their route forward obstructed by a very tall obstacle indeed. The General's "shortcut" ended in a fence! They could either turn back around or else perform what the *Brooklyn Daily Eagle* reporter called a "Brodie."

The use of the word *Brodie* to signify a wild leap or stunt had come from Steven Brodie, the native New Yorker who had allegedly jumped off the Brooklyn Bridge into the East River, apparently just to prove he could.[4] Rosalie and her suffragettes were left with no recourse but to Brodie over the fence now, the Brooklyn reporter teased, if they hoped to clear it. To do so they would have to do something considered entirely unladylike: straddle a fence with a huddle of male reporters hovering nearby. The General made the war correspondents promise they wouldn't take the "tiniest peek" while the pilgrims pulled their up-and-over.

It came off without a hitch but for a small tumble the General herself took upon dismount. Rosalie's army was well on its merry way now toward Sleepy Hollow, the spooky little town that had been the setting for Washington Irving's famous tale "The Legend of Sleepy Hollow." Irving had written of the village: "From the listless repose of the place, and the peculiar character of its inhabitants, who are descendants from the original Dutch settlers, this sequestered glen has long been known by name of Sleepy Hollow…. A drowsy, dreamy influence seems to hang over the land, and to pervade the very atmosphere."[5]

Rosalie Jones might have let herself be spooked, but only for just a moment. She could surely feel a slip of what Washington Irving felt here in the misty hills and dales created by the bends in the valley as it followed the river. This could indeed be a very eerie place, especially if you were Ichabod Crane, the lovelorn schoolmaster riding home alone to be chased by the Headless Horseman rumored to be the ghost of a decapitated soldier. At moments like these General Jones was perhaps more than usually glad for the companionship of the officers marching noisily behind her.

At Tarrytown General Jones's army marched toward a school for young girls. When the students saw Rosalie approaching, the girls ran out onto the lawn carrying a giant streamer bearing the name of their school: the Knox School. The General smiled at them and called out, "You are all going to have a vote," and they sent up a cheer.[6]

Shortly thereafter a delegation of women from Tarrytown arrived in automobiles to escort the marchers to the church where Jessie was to give one of her impassioned speeches.

As Rosalie introduced Jessie as the day's speaker, nearly one hundred boys from the nearby Irving School noisily took their seats under the watchful eye of their headmaster. Given that the school was named after Washington Irving, hopefully the schoolmaster wouldn't be traveling home at night alone across covered bridges!

Jessie spoke for nearly twenty minutes, inspired by a church packed to the rafters with avid listeners. She pointed out that the governments of the past had fallen not so much because of what everyday citizens had done or not done, but because the rich had failed in their duty to insist on equity for all citizens. She compared Rosalie's pilgrims to Native American messengers carrying vital words and sentiments from chief to chief. And in her grand finale she predicted that women would have the vote very soon. At that, the young people in the audience erupted in applause, with the grown-ups joining in shortly thereafter.

The Reverend Ashmead, the rector who had kindly offered the use of his church hall for Jessie's speech, was one of countless men, many of them behind the scenes in the clergy, who were then working on behalf of the suffrage cause — often at some considerable risk to their own careers. There were plenty of religious people who believed that the Bible taught the inferiority of women, and the men of the cloth who dared to suggest otherwise had earned Rosalie's respect. Reverend Ashmead was one of those brave religious men who had the courage to challenge his congregation when necessary.

Rosalie and her army exited the church hall to the sound of moving picture machines clicking away. That portions of their nascent march were being captured in moving pictures amazed her. Ten years ago the young General might have laughed had one of her college girlfriends told her she would be leading an all-women army on a march that would make them "film stars," but here it was. Predicting the future was a very fickle business indeed.

Still, Rosalie believed that Jessie was correct in what she had prophesied just now in the rectory — that soon women would have the vote in New York and across the nation. But if a mere ten years ago Rosalie couldn't imagine she'd be the star of someone's moving picture show, or that a moving picture show would exist at all, maybe it was possible that a decade from now there would be a woman senator from New York!

As the last of the army emerged into the cold out-of-doors, the girls of the Knox School formed a receiving line and raised their voices high into the wintry air with a cheer of their own design that went:

> Rah, rah, rah
> Do not fret
> You will get to Albany yet
> Ray, ray, ray
> Ret, ret, ret
> Cheer, cheer, cheer for the suffragette

Not to be outdone, the boys of the Irving School attempted their own cheer next, though the girls had caused such a hubbub with theirs that Rosalie could hardly make out the boys'. Suffice it to say that it, too, ended on the word "suffragette." It was good, Rosalie felt, for schoolboys to see what women were capable of, so that one day they might better understand their wife, if indeed they chose to have a wife, and her need for equality in her marriage and in her society. Seeing something was a powerful thing, the way Edison's moving picture machine had made believers out of the many who said pictures could never be animated.

"It is so hard to leave," Rosalie said when the boys' improvised cheer was through, and the call of the road beckoned once more. She shook the hands of the supporters crowding around the pilgrims and turned in the direction of their next stop: Ossining.

"Left! Left! Left!" she called out to bring her army back into order, and Lavinia piped up with her rallying cry, "Votes for women!" Rosalie hoped the reporters would fall into line, too, but of course they didn't. Shepherding newspaper writers was, the General was coming to learn, something like herding cats.

Rosalie now sent three scouts ahead to talk with representatives of the Sleepy Hollow Country Club who hoped to host the suffragettes that afternoon. The club was located halfway between Sleepy Hollow and Ossining to the north, making it the ideal midway point at which to stop for lunch. Unfortunately, there had been yet another mix-up in securing advance rations, and the club did not have enough food for both pilgrims and reporters. The reporters, of course, promptly found a bakery wagon and nearly bought out the baker's stock. Even so, some were still hungry, a point made abundantly clear when one of the war correspondents spotted a chicken and ran off after it, shouting, "Live off the land! Live off the land!" The journalist was joking, but the pangs were real.

Preoccupied as she was with obtaining food for her army, Rosalie couldn't help but be amused. What did these city reporters even know about the rural terrain they were now entering? Rosalie had at least the luxury of roaming across the countryside as a girl growing up on her family's Long Island estate. She knew enough, at least, to know it was a very difficult proposition indeed to catch a chicken! The reporters were in something of a snit today, as Mrs. Inez Craven and her headline-generating dog, Elizabeth, had dropped out of the hike, vowing that they would return as soon as possible.

To the extent that the reporters adored Inez, they did so because she kept liquor in her knapsack — "something mighty fine for snake bite" they called it — and because she would occasionally give them a sip in return for good behavior.[7] One reporter from the *Brooklyn Daily Eagle* complained that things were rather "dull" without Inez and "Liz," the suffrage terrier, but Rosalie and the officers in her pilgrim army appreciated the abundance of oxygen in the air now that attention-hungry Inez was not there to suck it all away. The same grumpy reporter from Brooklyn who bemoaned the loss of Inez, her dog, and her alcohol had counted dozens of "desertions" from the ranks since the women's army had left the Broadway and 242nd subway stop in the Bronx.

In any case, Rosalie had greater worries than the flighty boo-birds in the press corps, for she had an army to feed and water. Not far up the road the General spotted a sign that read "Meals served here" at a small roadside eatery where they could refuel their engines. Rosalie was accustomed to eating regular square meals, and on this, her second day of the march, she was almost startled by her body's capacity to register true hunger. Having lived in New York City for a number of years — where there was always a restaurant, delicatessen, or market right around the corner — she had forgotten that ready-made food could be much harder to come by in more rural places.

An hour later the reporters returned (after presumably eating their fill) and joined up with Rosalie's army again, whereupon someone took up the chant:

> Tramp, Tramp, Tramp
> The girls are marching![8]

But the improvised ditty didn't stick, and not long after the suffrage pilgrims were agitating for a new song. The trouble was, their tired brains could not generate any sufficiently clever lyrics, and this fact only seemed to further depress their flagging spirits.

"Mark time!" Rosalie ordered, hoping a quickening of the pace would help her army forget its discontentment and move double-time toward their goal. The General's order worked, and the marching pilgrims quickly left the journalists behind.

As they moved on, a man approached in a horse-drawn wagon. He stopped to ask about the spectacle before him. Clearly, he had never seen a column of female protesters on a march of nearly 175 miles, but then again, how many people in America could claim to have witnessed such a thing?

Rosalie called her column of troops to a halt and explained her cause to the man right there on the side of road. The impromptu lesson quickly turned into a small suffrage rally. This was exhilarating — exactly what Rosalie and Ida and Lavinia had dared to dream might happen when they began: inquisitive, open-minded men and women willing to learn the truth, straight from the horses' mouths, as it were!

This episode with the man in the wagon was soon followed by another roadside conversion experience, now with a woman on crutches. Apparently she was recovering from an illness, and her doctor had advised her that it would be healthful to get some fresh air. Having heard that the pilgrims were coming, she had asked the good doctor whether her fresh-air cure might consist of waiting for Rosalie's army.

"Do you believe in votes for women?" Colonel Craft asked the woman.

"I do," she said, and cheered and waved as the column marched by.

Ossining was now within reach. It had previously been known as Sing-Sing, but it had changed its name to distinguish itself from the massive state prison nearby. Rosalie thrilled at the sight of Ossining's Cliff Harmon when he appeared in his car, offering her weary army a bungalow in which to stay for the night.

As they marched into the town square, the air turned damp. The clouds had lowered and snow was looming. Rosalie had expected snow in New York in December, but the weather had been so thoroughly cooperative these first two days the prospect of plodding through powder had seemed a remote prospect until now. General Jones jumped atop the supply wagon and called for her troops to raise their suffragette battle cry: "Votes for women!" The sound of their voices brought the villagers who lived above the square to their windows.

Surveying the scene, Rosalie commented, as much to herself and her officers as to the reporters in tow, "And thence they marched ten parasangs." She added, "This is the suffragist Anabasis,"[9] referencing the book written by the great general Xenophon, the Greek who once led a forgotten platoon of ragtag soldiers from deep in enemy territory, across the mountains, to a triumphant arrival despite the steepest of odds. "We are going to do at least ten miles a day and we will not be daunted by the little snowstorm," the General continued.[10]

A fellow New Yorker, Mrs. Anna Ross Weeks, suffragist and poet, chimed in, "You men will be ashamed of yourselves if you don't vote for woman suffrage. We hear a lot of talk about the 'fairer sex,' but shouldn't you men be called the 'unfair sex'?"

Before long a crowd of two hundred had gathered to hear what the woman atop the wagon had to say for herself. A man hanging out of one of the windows cupped his hands so he could be heard above the din and shouted, "How about women going to war?"

"When battleships can fire projectiles three miles, being a soldier is not so brave a thing as it used to be," Rosalie declared.[11] "I would be more afraid of women who dropped a bomb from an airplane than I would a man."

CHAPTER 4:
HEARTACHES AND JAILBREAKS

No less an institution than the *New York Times* had written of the army's approach to Ossining, "The marching suffragists led by 'General' Rosalie Jones, stormed this place tonight, and after firing a volley from the public square and distributing much literature, scattered to their rest." Before she had gone to bed Rosalie had told the reporter that she was satisfied with the day's march, as indeed she had been.[1]

Now, though, the glorious, path-breaking headlines of the previous night seemed long past; the suffragettes had only one goal in mind: *Peekskill.* The evening's destination had become a mantra for the day's hike, a word whose two syllables seemed as if they might better serve as a marching rhythm for them: *Peeks-kill, Peeks-kill.* The place names of this rather remote region — Fishkill, Peekskill, even Catskill — might have sounded unnecessarily morbid to Rosalie as a girl growing up on Long Island until she had learned that the word *kill* meant "stream" in the language of the Dutch immigrants who had settled this area.

Still, Rosalie had good reason to indulge in some morbid thoughts. Her army had learned yesterday that there would be nowhere to eat on the day's march to Peekskill, thus the hike there would be "forced" — the word Rosalie had settled on after much thought — in that for the first time they would not stop. When word had gone through the ranks of the day's challenge, Rosalie's already diminished numbers had decreased to just three. Jessie Hardy Stubbs, her speechmaker-in-chief, had far too many engagements in New York City, and had left the march momentarily. (The fact that she had promised to return offered at least some small consolation.)[2] Katherine Abbot, their drummer, had long since gone home, leaving the platoon without music to buoy their spirits. Rosalie's last "private," Alice E. Smith, had temporarily left the march earlier in the morning, explaining that she had received an urgent message imploring her to return to New York City. Only Lavinia

"Little Doc" Dock and the ever-loyal Colonel Ida Craft remained, plus a smattering of the press. From the beginning Rosalie had told the press that only six of the trampers would hike all the way to capital, but now even that number seemed optimistic.

To make matters worse, rain had begun to fall, a steady drizzle that blurred the road before them and turned their woolen clothing into damp, itchy straightjackets. Rosalie led the way, as always, through fog so thick she could barely see her hands in front of her face.

The General's tone turned solemn. "The weather will not daunt us,"[3] she said to her two remaining officers. "We are going to Albany, and the road lies ahead." She knew, of course, how self-evident both these statements must have seemed to Ida and Lavinia at that moment, but she sensed, too, the need to say something definitive, lest the silence bespeak a hopelessness she did not intend. This, the third day of the epic march of the suffragettes, appeared as if it might be the most difficult yet.

"Votes for women!" Lavinia answered loudly, which was the Surgeon General's way of saying, *We're still with you, Rosalie. Lead on!*

Rosalie, Lavinia, and Ida tromped along silently, heads hung low against the cold and damp. It seemed, at least, that there were now more honks and hollers than ever before along the road to the capital. The sight of these dauntless women trudging through the mud, footsore and weary, had created a mood of compensatory gaiety that one of the reporters following the corps claimed had elicited a "continual ovation" from passersby. Time and again people shouted out words of encouragement. It was as if something deep in the human heart — something universal — reached out when it saw others enduring hardship and difficulty for a principle they so completely believed in.

The reporters had already begun to whisper among themselves, speculating that this would be the end, the Waterloo, of the marching suffragettes. They would bow out at Peekskill, the smart money said, and retreat to their warm beds. Rosalie, however, was committed to the cause, and vowed that she would continue, whatever the odds. Ida and Lavinia echoed the stalwartness of their general's sentiments.

But there was also a new cause for anxiety. Their morning "alarm" at Ossining had been the whistle from nearby Sing-Sing prison followed shortly thereafter by the grapevine news that Chester "Kid" Yates, a notorious criminal serving a twenty-plus year sentence for bank robbery, had escaped from the gloomy penitentiary. He was rumored to be haunting the very woods through which Rosalie's faithful pilgrims now walked. Yates was supposed to be in a "desperate mood," and he now had the cover of fog as his ally. Headlines had already declared it the "heaviest fog in many years," and reported on the fact that in many towns along the Great Lakes regular whistles had had to be sounded to serve as beacons just so the fishing boats could make it back to shore.[4]

The lack of available food meant Rosalie's army had no choice but to press on, but the knowledge that an escaped convict might be fleeing for his life somewhere in these heavily forested hills argued for caution. Perhaps it would be wise to delay the trip for a day to see if the hardened criminal could be apprehended. And yet if Rosalie's army did stop for fear of its own safety, its refusal to march would only confirm an ugly gender stereotype; the marchers would be caricatured in the press as timid women afraid of leaving for fear of meeting the Big Bad Wolf in the woods. Already reporters had filed stories in which they accused the marchers of only "pretending" to be undeterred by news of this fugitive.

So time-sensitive was the news of Yates's breakout that it had arrived to the *Kingston Daily Freeman* by telegraph directly from the prison. The report dubbed Chester W. Yates "one of the most daring thieves in the country" and the "brains behind a major bank heist.[5] He had only done six months of his sentence and already he had flown the coop. Sing-Sing warden John S. Kennedy and the other prison-keepers told the *Daily Freeman* they had "not the slightest idea" how Yates might have escaped.

"This is the first escape that has happened since I took charge here," said the warden. "And I cannot conceive how the man got away. He must have skipped out of line as the carpenter's shop crew were being led to work, but how he escaped unseen is more than I can say." The newspaper went on to say, "Yates possesses a remarkable career for a criminal of only twenty-nine years of age." "Kid" Yates was not much older than Rosalie!

If Yates possessed a remarkable ability to evade justice, Rosalie Gardiner Jones possessed a remarkable ability for visionary persistence, and so from the front of their small line she called for her troops to quicken their pace, fully intending to reach Peekskill by mid-afternoon and thus prove all the skeptics wrong. Rosalie was stiffer today than she had been on any day before, but as she walked she found the rust in her aching joints beginning to dissipate (perhaps aided by the foot treatments Lavinia had administered the previous night). But Lavinia herself was the one in need of treatment, with her feet so badly blistered she had to cut a hole in her shoe to make room for the swelling.

In the little village of Croton a woman called out "Good luck!" to the pilgrims from the steps of her house, and waved energetically. "I am in favor of you!" said the woman, who introduced herself as Emma.[6]

"If you are with us," Ida called back, never one to miss an opportunity, "sign this application for membership to the suffrage society." The Colonel stuck the application in Emma's hands, and Emma signed. Impressed, Rosalie invited Emma to march along with them for the remainder of that day's hike.

"Got to go get my husband's dinner," Emma said, disappearing back inside her house.

Clearly, Emma was a stand-up woman — someone who could be counted on to support the votes-for-women cause — and yet she did not seem to recognize the irony of her decision; she had just passed up a chance to join a historic march to do her solemn duty as a wife. Why couldn't the husband fix his own meal just this one day? And how could the suffragette army help a woman like Emma see that women's rights also meant more independence for women — more freedom of thought, of action, more relief from household drudgery and the many things that kept her exclusively at home rather than out doing good in her community. Most Antis like Rosalie's mother would claim Emma had made the only proper decision — to look after her family's needs first and foremost. But what if a woman's sacred obligations — to her family, to her community, and to herself — needn't always be in conflict? What if a woman could attend to all three *and* whatever else she cared to give her time and attention to?

The road to Peekskill amounted to a roller coaster — up and down, right then left. A man from Croton by the name of Charles showed up with his two twin daughters, both four years of age, to say that he fully expected his girls would be able to vote when they came of age, and the pilgrims took heart in the sanctity and certainty of his declaration. Still, for these small encouragements, the road on the third day proved a long one, and Rosalie and her army had begun, in spite of themselves, to look eagerly for the road signs that counted down the distance to Peekskill.

As they neared town they saw a man with a horse-drawn wagon approaching them, and Rosalie called out "Halt!"

"Do you believe in the rights of women?" she asked.

The man had a piece of straw hanging from his mouth and seemed likely to say no. But then he stopped himself, leaned over, and replied coyly, "I do… sometimes."

"Complimentary but not convincing," Rosalie muttered as the man and his wagon team passed by. There was a certain class of men whose support was what Rosalie might best characterize as patronizing, and it wasn't just hayseeds in the country who engaged in such ostensible flattery. Rosalie didn't consider herself especially beautiful, but she had noticed that most men liked the pretty suffragettes best, or at least thought them the best representatives of their class. The General had marched with many others in Ohio to whom the jeering men wouldn't give the time of day, and yet the same men who dismissed the older women in the movement as crones would listen to her as a legitimate protester. The men who believed women were worthy of respect only to the degree to which they were beautiful were the worst of the lot.

Other men on the route made other "gentlemanly" gestures, which, while they weren't entirely boorish or insulting, still irked Rosalie. One such character, catching sight of an unused wheelbarrow parked in a nearby yard, had wheeled it over and said, "Ladies, will you have a ride? You must be tired of walking."

Rosalie was proud of the marchers as each of them, without saying a word, passed on the offer. Why did some feel the need to make a mockery of things they struggled to understand, as if laughter were a means of dismissing them? Men were constantly opening doors for women. Such gentlemanly gestures were all well and good, but if women wanted real independence they would, by and by, need to free men from the societal expectations that likewise shackled and imprisoned them.

Momentarily lost in her thoughts, Rosalie found herself first humming, then singing, the old hymn "Blest Be the Tie That Binds." The song was well over a century old, but it seemed strangely right for the occasion. One of the General's favorite verses went:

> We share each other's woes,
> Our mutual burdens bear;
> And often for each other flows
> The sympathizing tear.
> When we asunder part,
> It gives us inward pain;
> But we shall still be joined in heart,
> And hope to meet again.
> This glorious hope revives
> Our courage by the way;
> While each in expectation lives,
> And longs to see the day.[7]

As the song ended, a gaggle of overwintering geese at the side of the road commenced to honking in a tone that suggested irreverent laughter.

"And yet Rome was saved by geese," Rosalie commented, and the birds promptly stopped their squawking.[8]

The war correspondents complimented the General on her voice, which they said was remarkably in tune after so long and arduous a hike, but Rosalie would hear none of it. A voice was a thing everyone had. Like courage, it was there in reserve, saved for when it was truly needed.

"Peekskill is just before us now," Rosalie said, pointing excitedly to the trolley tracks leading into town. Ida and Lavinia peered into the misty foreground, trying to determine just how far it was into town. "Forward!" the General ordered, and as if by magic the suffrage delegation from Peekskill emerged like ghosts. They had arrived to walk with the pilgrims the remaining distance to Peekskill.

Cries rang out as the procession reached the edge of town. "The suffragettes are coming!" And when Rosalie's army arrived at the Raleigh Hotel where they would be staying for the night, they found a crowd already assembled, and another kindly policeman, who, like Police Chief Wolff in Yonkers, pledged his support for their cause.

When one of the war correspondents pointed out that the pilgrims had now walked forty-two miles from New York City, Rosalie's troops smiled in acknowledgment. They were too exhausted for words.

Tomorrow would be Fishkill — another twenty-two miles away, with snow and rain in the forecast, but already the General felt certain she might be coming down with a cold.

Rosalie hated to show weakness, for she knew many of the journalists would pitch her vulnerability as characteristic of her sex. Already one had pegged her ragtag band of soldiers as "weary and footsore" and further observed, tongue firmly in cheek, "The term 'small army,' is used simply to please the suffragettes. They do love that word 'army,' so no mention will be made here of the fact that they numbered only five or six."[9]

The same story — one of many national stories datelined "Peekskill, N.Y. December 20" — sounded more like a mean-spirited gossip column than pure reporting:

> General Jones acquitted herself splendidly and received many handsome compliments, but some of her less spartan followers showed the wear and tear of the trip. Even a suffragette has feelings, and how can one walk several days over New York country roads in winter without having those feelings stirred to their very depths?
>
> Well, as we were just saying, General Jones acted perfectly lovely as a commander.

"Comrades!" she said, addressing the army, "we have made gratifying progress. We will press on, will we not?"

(Suppressed groans. Several voices in undertone: "Yes we will NOT!" Still other voices: "Oh! my poor feet!...")

"ON to Albany!" was the audible reply. "WE WILL!"

Was the reporter correct — had Rosalie's faithful troopers ever really grumbled and complained as they left, or had the unnamed scribbler behind the byline merely exercised poetic license? Here was yet another article that seemed to delight in sowing discord in the ranks, to look for human flaws and failings rather than auspicious fates and good fortunes. Still, even this cynical treatment ended on a hopeful note, describing men who witnessed the sight of Rosalie's suffragettes on the march and found themselves conceding the army's unrivaled spirit in ways they never would have imagined, saying, "Aw! Let 'em have the vote if they want it that bad!"

✿　✿　✿

The following morning confirmed what Rosalie had previously feared: She had come down with a head cold. She imagined she must have looked a terrible sight when Ida and Jessie, the latter now returned to the march, found the General still wearing her knitted slippers and propped up woefully on a stack of pillows.

"How much farther to Albany?" asked Rosalie, though she posed the question with a wan smile that let the girls know she would somehow summon the energy to join them.[10]

A moment later the ailing General was on her feet again, searching for her knapsack and toothbrush. The toothbrush she located, but something else — something mission-critical — was nowhere to be seen. A mounting sense of desperation settled in the pit of the General's stomach. "The message," Rosalie heard herself say aloud in disbelief, then again, more loudly this time and to no one in particular, "It's gone!"

That startled utterance brought the General's second-in-command rushing to her aid. Together, she and Ida looked in vain for the scroll that, in a mere single page of parchment, represented the most practical point of the march: the message to the Governor-elect. The General and her colonel looked under and around the bed, in the drawers of the dressing table, in and around the armoire and nightstand. Even the bathroom was searched, but to no avail.

Soon the whole hotel was in chaos, searching high and low, anywhere and everywhere, for the message Rosalie had written in her own hand. Ida and Rosalie painstakingly retraced the General's steps from the night before, Rosalie inwardly cursing herself for her carelessness. After nearly a half hour of frantic searching, Ida recommended calling the police, but Rosalie disagreed, arguing that the parchment must still be in the inn somewhere, even though she hardly believed it herself. Besides, Rosalie could only imagine what the merciless, gossip-mongering headlines might read: "Scatter-brained General Misplaces Suffrage Magna Carta!" "Loose General Loses Litany of Demands; General Jones Hysterical Over Lost Suffrage Scroll."

No, Rosalie would most certainly not be calling the police. If she did, she might as well send a press release to the *New York Times* bearing the headline, "FOR IMMEDIATE RELEASE: Idiot General Disgraced!!!"

A half-hour of frenzied searching ensued before Lavinia returned to the hotel from her morning outing to join the search. And there, in Lavinia's haversack, they discovered the precious message! The General fairly screamed with relief, snatching the lost missive from Lavinia's hand while frantically checking to see that its seal remained unbroken. The whole idea had been to keep the contents of the message secret from the press and from casual bystanders and day-hikers; it was intended specifically, and privately, for the eyes of the Governor-elect only, and with fervent hope that he would then share it with the rest of the world.

Rosalie looked up from the still-sealed scroll to find Lavinia glaring at her from behind her glasses. The Surgeon General's wounded look said it all: She believed that Rosalie suspected her of sneaking a peek at the top-secret message!

Lavinia reddened, her wounded pride and growing indignation flushing her cheeks. Rosalie hastened to reassure the good nurse that it was only out of caution that she had checked the seal — she had, after all, been entrusted by the Central Committee to keep the message safe. She had no reason to suspect Lavinia of any breach of trust or disloyalty to the mission, she assured her.

Lavinia's softening demeanor told Rosalie that a confrontation with her oldest, most experienced officer had been narrowly averted. The march to Fishkill could proceed, but not before the General called a Council of War with her officers to apprise them of the latest conditions on the ground. Rosalie's bulletin consisted of two main items:

1) Rosalie would march on, illness be damned!
2) A telegram had been waiting for the General at the hotel informing her that Inez Craven had officially promised (or, to put it another way, threatened) to re-join the hike, along with her British flag, her cigarettes, her alcohol, and her African terrier.

Inez would also be bringing with her a violent brand of suffrage that Rosalie, even in her passions, found difficult to stomach. Mrs. Craven, like many of her British and European counterparts, believed that it was as useful to burn down a barn as to give an impassioned votes-for-women speech from one. Even many Britons had come to prefer the more law-abiding nature of the American votes-for-women movement. "It is comforting to see the dignified and far more efficient mien of American suffragettes," observed one commentator, "and more power to their arm!" This same observer put it still more plainly elsewhere in the article, adding, "We should distinguish between the suffragette and the militant suffragette; the former is a reasonable being demanding justice; the latter is a species of wild beast."[11]

Rosalie circled up with her officers, watching them closely as she revealed each piece of new information. The first declaration — that she would march despite her health — was met with great cheer; the second —regarding Inez's threatened rejoining of the march she had abandoned — was greeted with universal condemnation. There was no place among the army's stalwart officers for quitters, and there was no place for violence in a nonviolent march.

Rosalie returned to the headline-hungry journalists with the officers' verdict. Mrs. Inez Craven was not welcome, thank you very much, and if the notorious British suffragette dared try to throw herself and her unsavory methods at their determined little band, they would resist with all due force.

Inez may have her prettily ribboned suffrage dog, but Rosalie and her army knew how to bite when occasion called.

CHAPTER 5:
EVEN GENERALS
HAVE MOTHERS

———————————

It was all Rosalie could do to make her way to the men's banquet in Fishkill to say a few words of thanks to supporters before turning the speechmaking over to Jessie. Lavinia and Ida had stayed behind at the Hotel Holland; after the day's twenty-two mile hike through snow and ice and up a mountain, they were exhausted, and it seemed only fair that they should rest.

Jessie rose to accept the kind words of the toastmaster of the event, following on the heels of a half dozen male speakers.[1] Jessie merely hoped that the suffragettes were something more than a novelty to these men, and that they might sincerely be converted. In any case, the setting evidenced greater decorum than had the previous night's speaking engagement at the Colonial Theater in Peekskill, where Jessie's votes-for-women speech had followed the gyrations of a lady leopard tamer. (And to think that people found marching suffragettes exotic!)

With Jessie standing before him now, the jolly master of ceremonies picked up a basket of holly and presented it with great flourish and a host of compliments to her with all good wishes for a safe and speedy journey. The Fishkill banqueters rose to their feet at this, and Jessie did her best to find an appropriately generous reply.

"Mr. Toastmaster.... I accept this token of your undertaking... in the name of my sister pilgrims, all of whom I wish might be here and return every generous thought you have for us."

The pilgrims were indeed grateful. It had been the most difficult day of hiking yet — a full twenty-two miles! Rosalie, for her part, had trudged the entire distance in rubber boots padded with cotton courtesy of her surgeon general.

The "little General," as the newspapers had taken to calling Rosalie, had talked tough at the start of the day. In part, she supposed she was hoping to distract attention from her illness and the fiasco back at the hotel. Whatever the reason, the day's mounting obstacles had revived her wartime spirits, and General Jones was in a fighting mood. Rosalie had, perhaps foolishly, issued a challenge to any Antis who wanted to confront her army at the side of the road. She and her band were ready to defend publicly their cause, anytime and anywhere. Then she said something even more headstrong, which she would later come to regret: "I wish they would come."

But when the reporters had dispersed and the need for tough talk had passed, she confessed to Lavinia just how hard it was to summon the willpower to go on while feeling so poorly, her body aching and shivering. Surgeon General Dock, who always seemed to have something useful to say in times of trouble and who was eager to make amends after the lost scroll incident, told the General the story of a soldier who managed to march an impossibly long distance by naming his feet, then coaxing them forward by name as if they were a team of reluctant horses. In so doing he had been able to forget his weariness.[2]

Lavinia's anecdote brought a smile to the General's face, and, after a bit of thought, she was inspired, and decided to name her feet "Percy" and "Meredith" after two of her friends.

"Percy" and "Meredith" had seen plenty in the past twenty-two miles on the way to Fishkill — suffrage babies wrapped in red, white, and blue bunting shown to the Rosalie's army by mothers in full support of the suffragettes' cause; tidy schoolhouses flying the American flag staffed by teachers who were nevertheless disinclined to agree with votes for women. The pilgrims had also been joined briefly by two "privates" from local organizations who walked with them and seemed to bring clearer and drier weather.

On a bluff overlooking the Hudson at Garrison, General Jones had thought it proper to pay homage to West Point Military Academy across the river. At Cold Spring, north of the academy, a Dr. and Mrs. Giles had turned out to join the marchers for a spell, though the joy they brought was tempered somewhat by a fierce west wind near Storm King Mountain. The pilgrims had tried to start a hopeful song, but the gale had blown it away, along with any comfort the tune might otherwise have provided. The wind had blown so hard that it drove the women behind their supply-wagon for shelter. For a frightening few minutes it had felt as if God himself had reared up and said no to the suffrage cause. None of the pilgrims had made any attempt at conversation, not until the winds finally subsided and a baker's wagon arrived, full of pastries and goodies — a rare moment of grace.

There had been other small moments of good fortune on the day's sojourn, including a group of men laboring along the road who had stopped to wish them luck. So, too, had there been a boat full of workers crossing the Hudson River, whose captain had sounded his whistle in such an unexpected salute that it brought tears to Rosalie's eyes and a reply of "God bless you."[3]

When they had first arrived at Fishkill at 7:00 p.m., Rosalie had gone immediately to bed, foregoing dinner, only to remerge later to accept the key to the city from the mayor. But before any of that, and before the pilgrimage's most difficult hike to date had begun, Rosalie had sent two messages. In the first, she tried to convince her mother that she was well enough to continue the march. In the second, she assured the National Woman Suffrage Association meeting in Chicago of her forward progress. The night before Rosalie dispatched her missive, Dr. Anna Howard Shaw, national president of that association, had told the convention of suffragists gathered in Chicago's Orchestra Hall, "We have had too much father. What we need is a little mother to offset the evil of too much fathering."[4] Perhaps it was so, but General Jones felt she could do with a little less mothering, or at least less of the kind of mothering Mary Jones supplied!

Now, as she readied herself for much-needed sleep, General Rosalie Jones hoped her missive would be enough and that her strong-willed, anti-suffragist mother would do what she had never once done before: retreat.

In the meantime, she'd proclaimed to the war correspondents and the rest of the Doubting Thomases in the press corps her every intention to "walk the rest of the way or die in the attempt."[5] The declaration may have sounded unnecessarily headstrong, but it was surely nothing next to the latest tactics from her sister suffragettes in Britain, who had just sabotaged phone lines in London to hold the population there hostage to their revolutionary cause.[6]

One of the war correspondents had written of the women of Fishkill: "There were many goodbyes spoken in Fishkill but little encouragement. Apparently the women of that place who believe in votes for women live on the side streets."[7]

Side streets indeed! Well, Rosalie's army couldn't expect a heroine's welcome in every village and hamlet, and, if nothing else, Jessie had been well received by the businessmen at the banquet. No matter. Yesterday they had tramped twenty-two miles, and now they were on their way to Wappingers Falls. Onward to bigger and better things!

Rosalie had allowed her footsore pilgrims to sleep in for the first time on their pilgrimage. While her loyal troops earned some badly needed rest, Rosalie wired ahead to Wappingers Falls, where they were to be guests of honor at that community's annual dance. "A little salve and a lot of witch hazel," she said, "and we'll dance you Wappingers to death."[8] When the war correspondents came calling, looking for their daily quotes, Rosalie assured them that the rubbing alcohol she'd put on her joints "had done wonders" and that today's sojourn would be "nothing but a little jaunt."[9]

"They are going to give a ball in our honor at Wappingers Falls tonight," she told the eager newshounds sniffing for a story, adding poignantly, "and we are all going to dance."

But when they assembled just before noon for the day's advance on Wappingers Falls eight miles distant, the discussion centered less on the Cinderella ball scheduled for later that evening and more on the marchers' feet. They were all swollen and blistered. Feet had become the primary topic of discussion when the army wasn't spreading the gospel of votes for women.[10]

When they were feeling especially brave or chatty, they would talk in nervous tones and under their breath about the escaped criminal Chester "Kid" Yates and the all-out manhunt underway for him in the forests surrounding the road on which they walked. Rosalie, Ida, and Lavinia only hoped "The Kid" had crossed over to the other side of the Hudson, and from there made a beeline west — that is, away from the pilgrims and deeper into the Adirondack Mountains.

Lavinia now walked with an almost permanent limp. And yet Rosalie was continually amazed that this remarkable woman, scholar, and nurse — some twenty-five years her senior — could keep up with her and Ida. Whenever Rosalie or Ida complained of an ailment, Lavinia would take out her first-aid kit and do whatever was necessary to mend the broken. Hers was a nurse's instinct — to heal — and it made not just Lavinia but also other healthcare workers ideal soldiers in the movement. It required deep empathy, the General appreciated now more than ever, to be able to walk a mile in someone else's shoes as well as to understand their needs and wants from the inside out. She might only have wished more men would volunteer for jobs like nursing and teaching — the helping professions. Perhaps it would deepen their compassion.

Like most gifted caregivers Lavinia was more accustomed to caring for others than being cared for. Twice on the march she had mentioned the presence of painful rocks in her shoes, but pride prevented her from asking Rosalie and Ida to slow their pace. Finally, Rosalie had ordered the march to a halt so that Lavinia could remove the impediments. When the General looked back over her shoulder later, she was gratified to see that Lavinia's limp had lessened.

Ida continued to provide comic relief, so earnest was she in her desire to spread information about the cause. Today, as they entered one of the more remote sections of their hike, Ida had decided to write a special circular she could give to the tramps said to frequent these woods. Who would feel more dispossessed or downtrodden than the vagrants who moved from town to town, without a home or a bed they could call their own? Men like John D. Rockefeller, Jay Gould, and John Archbold of Standard Oil had grown rich enough to build mansions in the handsome river valley around them, while the population of wandering poor grew by the day. This fact seemed counterintuitive to the pilgrim suffragettes; if America's richest were doing so well, why should not a rising tide float all boats?

In fact, the press had called Rosalie's army "trampers," too, for that, in effect, is what they had become. So in deciding to distribute her circulars to the vagrants en route, Ida supposed she would simply be one variety of tramp reaching out to another. When she had finished composing her original leaflets earlier that morning, the headline read: "Tramps are not all bad." And now, resting on an embankment ahead of Rosalie's army, was a man who looked the part.

"My friend," said Ida, bustling to his side in the way only she could bustle, "read this!" Ida looked very much pleased with herself as she handed him her leaflet. But as the army marched further down the road, they turned around to find the vagrant laughing heartily.

"Who is that man?" an incredulous Ida asked one of the locals.

"Him?" he replied. "Why, he owns a good part of the county."

At that news Colonel Craft frowned mightily, then tore up the remainder of her "tramp circulars." Sometimes Ida's enthusiasm for the cause got the better of her. Surely, there was an important lesson to be learned here that boiled down to the old adage about never judging a book by its cover. Antis were forever judging suffragettes, for example. They would look at a nicely dressed, college-educated young woman loudly protesting this or that injustice in the streets, and think, "Another of our girls posing as a representative of the lower classes." While it was true that many of the suffragettes came from well-to-do families, Rosalie had met many activists who had little more than the clothes on their backs and a burning desire to right a societal wrong.

Teachers offered another case study in false assumptions; this Rosalie knew for certain. Almost every day, the hike would take them past one or two schoolhouses. The teachers, who were often well-connected in the community, usually knew that the pilgrims were coming, and to their credit they arranged to have the General's army pay a classroom visit, or at least for the children to be on the playground as the women passed by on their historic march. Rosalie had hoped, *assumed* might be a better word, that schoolteachers — and they were nearly always young women — in the rural communities through which they passed would be the most forward-thinking, pro-women voices in town; but she had been wrong.

Take earlier that day, for example. They had come upon a country school and collectively decided that they would pay the children there a visit. Miss Elizabeth Livingstone, the teacher, had been just as surprised as the children at the visit from the group, but she welcomed them all the same. Rosalie asked the boys in Miss Livingstone's class if they were in favor of their mothers and sisters voting, and a small voice in the corner of the class replied politely, "Yes, Ma'am."

Lavinia looked at him and predicted that one day this boy would be president, and the boy, hearing that weighty prophecy, looked more worried than pleased. When they asked the boy's teacher, however, how she felt about the prospect of women voting, she demurred, saying she wasn't so sure but would study the matter further.

Ida, of course, made sure the teacher had plenty of literature to study over the long winter to come!

And it wasn't just Miss Livingstone. Ida had come up against several other naysayers that day. In one instance she had been stuffing a mailbox full of her circulars when she heard an angry man's voice screaming, "Women ain't got no right to vote!"

He had accused Ida of the federal offense of "tampering with the mail," and threatened to send her straight to the police.

Rosalie had had to halt the march to rescue Ida from the man's wrath. Whereas Ida's was an easily excitable, exuberant sort of energy, Rosalie's was a measured calmness, and after speaking with the man for some time, the General had him nearly turned around to her way of thinking. He had agreed, at least, to consider the votes-for-women question further, and had forgiven Ida for trespassing in his mailbox.

They had notched one possible convert for the day!

For others, though, no amount of argument would do. Some could not be convinced, Rosalie knew, though this basic truth was harder for Ida to accept. In the tiny town of Hughsonville, for example, it seemed the whole town had shown up to see the women foot soldiers, though the "whole town" in this case consisted mostly of the village clerk, the police department, and a bevy of what the war correspondents called "the village cut-ups," who would as soon ridicule suffragists as listen to them. Then there was Mrs. Hester Lawson, who lived just a few doors down from the town grocery, and who told the war correspondents, "A woman should be home with the children. If she hasn't any, let her borrow some. Lord knows there are enough to go around."

Mrs. Lawson's criticism was a familiar one, and it was a stereotype of course. The Antis were always trying to paint the suffragettes as a different class of woman entirely — one that concerned itself mainly with selfish pursuits and eschewed the responsibilities of family. It was the old scare tactic again — that there was something dangerous about an unmarried woman, in particular, who reached her mid- to late twenties, as Rosalie had, without finding a husband and bearing children. At times the accusations of these Antis against younger single women activists could feel almost like a witch hunt, and had the potential to make Rosalie and her friends feel like attitudes hadn't changed much since colonial Massachusetts in 1692.

For Jessie it was different; she was married and could talk to married women in a way Rosalie and Ida simply could not. In the eyes of many women in the towns through which they passed, marriage represented a kind of credential; it earned you a measure of respect, and yet at the same time it seemed to be a way of telling young women that they were only worth listening to if they were wed. Marriage often made women dependent, legally and otherwise, to the point that when the men in their lives moved on or passed on, society did not know how to regard them properly as individuals.

This very week in Ida's hometown newspaper, the *Brooklyn Daily Eagle*, a story headlined "Double Crime Due to Pride"[11] had run alongside news of the suffragettes' march. In California a young Japanese-American bride had killed herself and murdered her son because her husband had died two months earlier. After affixing her year-old baby to her breast, she had plunged a family heirloom dagger into her chest rather than endure the indignity of accepting care from another family. Had she been able to support herself and her son without a husband, such a needless tragedy could no doubt have been avoided.

And what had marriage really come to mean? A day after the women had begun their hike up Broadway, the *Brooklyn Daily Eagle* had reported the curious case of fifteen-year-old Mary Bub, who told a judge in the Children's Court that she had secretly married a Spanish firefighter by swearing to be eighteen. And yet Mary Bub could not remember either the name of the church or the minister who had married her.[12]

Alongside that article had run the still more chilling headline "B'Klyn Woman's Throat Cut," which told the gruesome tale of a newlywed married for only four months when her husband slashed her throat. The report refused the victim so much as her maiden name, referring to her only by "Mrs." followed by the surname she had been forced to take from the man who had taken her life.

Indeed, sometimes Rosalie and Ida wondered if the camaraderie enjoyed among married women amounted instead to a kind of commiseration; perhaps these married women wanted to be sure that the suffragettes had endured the same struggles in matrimony as they had, misery loving company. For her part, Rosalie thought she might like to marry one day, but for now she was entirely focused on her cause. Indeed, if she had married any of the men who had courted her thus far, would she be here now, leading the march? Probably not. Had she said yes to her earlier beaus, her efforts would more likely be centered around her would-be husband than around the health and welfare of womankind overall.

These and other thoughts occupied the General as she hiked at the head of what the newspapers had begun to call her "little band." By now the marching had become second nature. It was hard, sometimes, to prevent one's mind from wandering, from thinking ahead to the destination rather than focusing on the journey.

It was during just such a moment when Rosalie, at the head of her corps of woman soldiers, spotted the distant "skyline," if one could call it that, of the little town of Wappingers Falls. Her heart raced. Tonight they would have a square meal, a good rest, and a fine dance at the O'Rourke's Academy of Music.[13] They would finally be able to wear their gowns.

It was, they were told, the society event of the entire year for the village on the banks of the creek. Today they had hiked nearly nine miles on roads that had firmed up nicely after the recent rains, and had done so in almost record time. And now, under a cloudy but nevertheless dry sky, here it was: the day's destination within reach! From the ranks came a new marching song. "Well, here we are, well here we are," they sang over and over, the happy little tune adding a spring to their step before they altered their cry to "Albany or bust!"[14]

The strange elation they felt at that moment was indescribable until General Jones spied a figure walking rapidly toward the army from the direction of town. One of the Wappingers Falls welcome committee coming to greet them?! Rosalie narrowed her eyes and squinted into the distance at the silhouette of a figure whose gait looked strangely familiar to her. Yes, it was an older man for sure, walking alone — the head of the local Men's League for Equal Suffrage come to support their cause, Rosalie hoped.

Suddenly the General felt herself take a sharp inward breath.

Dr. O'Connor? It couldn't be — and yet it was, heaven help her!

Rosalie's mother — her overweening, anti-suffragist of a mother — had sent the family doctor all the way from New York City, presumably to force Rosalie to return home with him.[15]

Anger and embarrassment built swiftly inside the General until they threatened to overtake her. This was simply intolerable! General Jones whispered to her comrades the identity of the coming man, and together they hastily conceived a strategy to deal with the approaching threat. Of course this wasn't Dr. O'Connor's doing, bless him. He was only following orders from the family matriarch.

If Rosalie stopped now, within sight of town, she realized she was more vulnerable to forced abduction than she would be in a public place like the hotel, where the war correspondents, now lagging behind, and the local suffrage representatives would surely prevent Dr. O'Connor from taking her against her will.

Referring to Rosalie as "Miss Gardiner," Dr. O'Connor informed the General in the most soothing tones that her mother had read in the newspapers of the horrid conditions the army was facing on their wintry hike, and had insisted that her daughter come home at once, lest her stubborn head cold turn into life-threatening pneumonia. It was necessary for her health that she return to Long Island to spend Christmas with her family, the good doctor insisted

"I am walking to Albany," Rosalie told the family physician, firmly as ever. "And you may go right home and tell mother so."

Dr. O'Connor could be a very convincing man, but Rosalie kept walking, setting her sights on the Rush Hotel just up ahead. She would be there in a minute, and dared the medic to follow her inside.

Thankfully, at that moment the village president, Mr. Heaton, and the chief of police, Mr. Mara, appeared to escort the army the final distance into town, and only just in the nick of time. Of course, Dr. O'Connor followed at her heels into the hotel, clucking in the General's direction like a persistent father hen until Rosalie, utterly exhausted, fell wearily into the chair in the lobby of the hotel. She told the physician that she would absolutely hear no more of it until she had had time to get some dinner and better consider her reply. Dr. O'Connor replied in turn that he was afraid to return to Mrs. Jones without having accomplished his task. "I will never desert the cause," Rosalie reaffirmed to the doctor, springing from her chair with an energy that surprised her.[16]

In the meantime Ida volunteered to take the suffrage message to the Governor if Rosalie was forced home against her will. Lavinia made the same offer, but the General reminded them both that she was no quitter, and that she would be with them till the end, no matter what kind of trickery or obstructionist tactics her strong-willed, anti-suffragist mother employed.

After a brief meeting it was decided that Rosalie would write a formal message in reply, in a manner befitting the general of a noble army. Hers would be a war dispatch, and it would say simply that she was in reasonably good health and that she and her army would press on to the capital. Dr. O'Connor, in his role as go-between and courier, would return to New York City with the consolation message rather than with the intended prisoner of war. "I shall go to Albany," the General insisted. "The cause needs me; it is more important than my health, and I'll go or die."[17]

Dear Dr. O'Connor protested, of course, but with speeches needing giving and "Votes for women!" being shouted loudly by supporters, who likewise sent up the cry, "Eighty more miles to Albany!" the physician at last demurred, forced to accept the consolation prize of a dinner with Rosalie's army before returning home with the war dispatch and word that the suffragette General was at least in good enough health to resist capture. Jessie had the suffragist supporters riled up as ever, and to take Rosalie by force with their sympathies so roused would be next to impossible. The good doctor had underestimated the size and strength of Rosalie's newfound network of friends and supporters.

The war correspondents crowded around the General now, eager for the details of the dust-up. "Mother doesn't understand the importance of this campaign," she said, informing them that she had sent O'Connor politely but firmly back to the city. "She thought that I was footsore and weary and ruining my health but such reports are untrue. The cause needs me and I must go on."

Once she had confirmed reports from her scouts that Dr. O'Connor had in fact left town as promised, the General began to relax and ready herself for the night's dance at the Academy of Music. The truth was, she didn't feel much like dancing after everything she had been through that day, and neither did Ida or Lavinia. The same *Chicago Tribune* that faithfully reported the progress of Rosalie's army also ran headlines from London, where suffrage of the kind practiced by Mrs. Inez Craven had turned desperate, further darkening the pilgrims' mood. In London, votes-for-women militants had sabotaged the mail, using blood-red and black ink to obliterate addresses on Christmas cards in an attempt to cause holiday havoc and thereby draw greater attention to their cause.[18]

At Wappingers Falls everybody who was anybody in the entire county attended the event the newspapers had billed as "the most exclusive society function of the season."[19] Rosalie's army served as guests of honor at the Assembly Dance, and the ballroom swelled with all the who's who of the Hudson Valley — over three hundred who's whos in fact — including a large contingent from Vassar. Students from Princeton, Yale, Williams, and Amherst attended as well, spilling across the overflowing dance floor and filling the room. The only thing that competed with the music was the laughter.

Jessie danced with abandon. She was a grand dancer, and having recently returned from yet another trip back to New York City, was much better rested than the "pilgrims three" — Rosalie, Ida, and Lavinia. Reporters commented to each other about the jealousy that the other women seemed to feel as they watched Jessie whirl on the dance floor, but it didn't last long. Someone needed to dance, speak cleverly, and have energy left at the end of the day to socialize and carry on, and if it couldn't be the beleaguered army officers, they were glad Jessie was along to fulfill the General's pledge that the marching suffragettes would "dance the Wappingers to death."

A movement such as theirs positively required diverse talents, even when that talent was dancing!

By 1:30 a.m. the suffragettes had danced as much as their blistered feet would allow, and still they fairly floated across the floor until the strains of the song "Home, Sweet Home" signaled the night's last dance and the army's need to return to its hotel. Cinderella may have waltzed till the stroke of midnight (and likewise suffered an overdemanding mother) but Rosalie and her army had just gone Cinderella two hours better, for the hotel clocks read 2:00 a.m. as the tired pilgrims fell wearily, but happily, into bed.

CHAPTER 6:
LETTERS FROM THE FRONT

Jessie struggled to get herself out of bed while her sister suffragettes slept soundly in their adjoining hotel rooms. Jessie had promised to pay a visit to the textile factory in Poughkeepsie, where the women began each day at 6 a.m. sharp.

Jessie was not a working girl, but she was a hard worker; this was a difference she and the other suffrage pilgrims were determined to honor. Jessie was free to travel back and forth from New York City while acting in her capacity as the suffragettes' war correspondent and press agent, but these garment workers reported to the overalls factory each and every morning at the same godforsaken hour, rain or shine, to do the work that needed doing. It was the least Jessie could do for a single morning to share in their toil while the officers of the regular army took their hard-won rest.

Ida, however, had insisted on coming along, and now followed on Jessie's heels like an eager puppy. The factory women were still rubbing sleep from their eyes when Jessie climbed atop one of the workbenches and began to preach the votes-for-women gospel, until she saw the president of the company, Mr. John M. Gering, walking rapidly toward her, his face twisted into what appeared to be a look of abject consternation.

"This won't do!" he proclaimed loudly as Jessie looked down at him from atop the bench, feeling a bit sheepish.[1]

All around her Jessie could feel the women workers of the garment factory stiffen, no doubt wondering what would happen next.

"Why not, Sir?" Jessie asked.

"Because they can't hear you!" the president said, giving the order for the factory machinery to be shut down while Jessie spoke her peace.

Thanking Mr. Gering, Jessie looked out at the crowd of expectant workers and spoke from the heart. She told them that they were entering a female century during which women would indeed win the vote and come to oversee many aspects of life previously controlled by men.

So moved was Colonel Craft by Jessie's early-morning speech on behalf of the cause, Ida resolved to give one of her own. She echoed Jessie's impassioned plea, explaining how much better all women — not just workers — would be once they had won the ballot. Jessie and Ida spoke with such passion and conviction that when they were through, the women of the factory cheered, gathered together in a kind of informal congress, and decided to give up half a day's pay to walk along with Rosalie's army to Poughkeepsie. "Every mother's daughter in the factory enlisted in the cause," wrote one of the war correspondents who'd come along to the factory that morning.[2]

And further, the factory workers informed the surprised and humbled Jessie and Ida that they had sewed each of the pilgrims a pair of overalls as a keepsake and a souvenir by which they could one day remember their historic march. It was obvious overalls wouldn't do to walk in, so the garment workers sewed them in miniature, such that they could be pinned to the marchers' knapsacks as mementos.

✿　✿　✿

Later, back at the hotel, Rosalie and her officers found themselves in the midst of their first real argument of their journey, and Rosalie was crying. The tears no doubt made her feel small, stupid, and childish, but she couldn't stop them from falling. She had always been this way, stoical in the face of threats and obstacles, but with a tipping point that, when reached, gave way to strong emotion. And that's how she felt now — caught between the desire to be a dutiful daughter who loved and wanted to please her mother, and her obligations to her friends and their shared cause.

In front of her lay a telegram from her mother, Mrs. Mary Elizabeth Jones, saying she would arrive tomorrow to take her daughter back. What an embarrassment it was to have a family feud made so painfully public. Already the Brooklyn newspaper had labeled Rosalie, through the eyes of her mother, a "disobedient child," and further suggested that her mother had threatened to "disinherit her" if Rosalie didn't quit the journey "at once."[3] They had also called her "obdurate," whatever that meant.

Ida paced back and forth in front of Rosalie now, offering little sympathy. Instead she saw fit to issue a sharp reminder, as she had the day before, that if the General dared quit, Ida, her second-in-command, would take over and deliver the message to the Governor without her! Through her tears Rosalie frowned deeply at her unrelenting colonel. "You're horrid, Ida. Mother or no mother, I am going on!"[4] Rosalie pulled on her hiking boots and met Ida and Lavinia and a local young woman, Miss Mary Lynch, who had approached them asking to be their flag-bearer for the day's march into Poughkeepsie from Wappingers Falls. General Jones wiped her eyes, and, determined, set off for Poughkeepsie with her followers close behind.

"If you desert, Rosalie," Ida reminded her, "I will carry the message alone."

Ida's persistent belligerence in turn angered Surgeon General Dock, who was sufficiently upset that the Colonel had so little faith in Rosalie's ability to resist her mother. She reminded Ida and Rosalie both that if there was any backing down at all, then *she* would be the one carrying the suffrage scroll to the Governor. She was, after all, the eldest and most experienced.

The previous night's ball had all but danced the discord from Rosalie's mind, but now, in the cold light of day, she felt the bitter sting of her mother's betrayal all over again. Dr. O'Connor had left Wappingers Falls yesterday evening, full from the consolation dinner to which the pilgrims had treated him, but otherwise empty of the promise of his purpose. He had warned Rosalie upon leaving that Mrs. Mary Jones might next take matters into her own hands and come to fetch her "unruly" daughter all by herself.

The news cast a pall over the day's hike ahead, but it could not dim the more hopeful news: Today's march would be a relatively short one at just under ten miles; the hikers would cross the halfway point today on their way to Albany; and, finally and most importantly, reinforcements would arrive in the form of a platoon of Vassar College suffragettes, who were to meet Rosalie's army five miles beyond Wappingers Falls and from there escort them into Poughkeepsie, where the votes-for-women debate had reached a fever pitch.

Vassar professors Laurie Wylie and Abbie Leach would join them as well in Poughkeepsie, where the pilgrims were scheduled to speak with the students of the women's college about their journey. How wonderful it must be, Rosalie allowed herself to think, to have woman professors involved. The General had had very few female professors when she'd attended college in Brooklyn. Only in women's colleges like Vassar, and in a few specialized departments such as nursing and sociology and teaching, were women professors at all common.

The trouble was, Vassar professors such as Professor Chamberlain had reported interest in suffrage to be declining rather than increasing, even among their all-female student body. Rosalie considered this fact a great irony and wondered why it should be so.

Still, it made some sense. Many of the young women enrolled at Vassar had been sent there to get an education that was really more of a membership card; their mothers and fathers believed they needed it as a prerequisite to join the fashionable class, the smart set. Women's colleges had to be careful not to embrace the suffrage movement too heartily for fear of angering traditional parents who didn't like the idea of paying good money to have their daughters turned into willful social agitators. Suffragettes, in their eyes, had an awfully hard time finding a job — not to mention a husband.

Young women received so many messages that turned them away from the votes-for-women cause, and it seemed that nearly everyone and everything conspired to put them on a conventional path. Even the so-called "progressive" press often printed stories that nudged women ever closer to orthodox roles. Just that day, for example, there had been an article in one of the newspapers covering the hike whose headline trumpeted, "Wellesleyites Welcome Stork."[5] Apparently, the alumnae of the renowned Massachusetts women's college had produced more babies since its inception than rival Holyoke, as if baby-making and baby-birthing were contests won by sheer volume! Wellesley women, the news reporters glowed, were especially fertile; the school's fifteen hundred or so alums had produced more than four thousand babies among them!

Who even kept track of such ridiculous statistics? Having a little bundle of joy was decidedly not at the top of General Jones's agenda at the moment, any more than it was for most generals engaged in battle. High on Rosalie's priority list right now was continuing the march into history, and Poughkeepsie. And in the meantime she hoped — desperately and truly hoped — that the woman who had given birth to her would respect her war dispatch and cease meddling in her affairs. If there was one thing on earth that irked generals more than anything, it was being told what to do by their mothers!

Fortunately, not far into their day's hike to Poughkeepsie, a small contingent of students enrolled in the local school for the deaf — Ben, Charles, and Joseph — turned out to issue their well-wishes. They had walked three miles to show their support in sign language, so Colonel Craft asked them, "Are you for votes for women?" Interpreted, their message was clear: "We are with you; good luck, and on to Albany!"[6] In reply to their good-spirited affirmation Colonel Craft did what Colonel Craft did best: She distributed votes-for-women literature to the boys and thanked them for their kind support.[7]

Not long afterward Rosalie again called her troops to a halt at Brookland Farms, where two farmers, Mr. and Mrs. Kirk, insisted that the marchers stop for sandwiches and tea.[8] The Kirks had been in favor of votes for women for twenty years, they said, and invited the pilgrims into the house for fresh doughnuts and cool milk. Alphonse, the pilgrims' supply-car driver, was so appreciative of the farm-fresh milk he drank his own personal record: eleven full glasses![9]

Two miles below the little village of Camelot a boy appeared on the side of the road determined to get General Jones's attention. His name was Jimmy, he said, and his father, the town barber, had sent him with an important message for the hikers. And yet Jimmy was so awestruck to be in Rosalie's presence that he struggled to get the words out, and when they did come, they came sheepishly. "Pop says that any of you that wants a shave, why, you can have it for nothing."[10] Rosalie's army burst out laughing. They *could* probably use a shave, but who had time for such superficialities?! Rosalie thanked the boy for his and his father's kind offer, explaining that they could use votes for women even more than they could use smooth skin.

True to her promise Professor Abbie Leach met Rosalie's army five miles south of Poughkeepsie with a detachment of one hundred students from Vassar women's college. The young women gave the General and her troops their most boisterous reception yet.[11] How heartening it was to see the sheer strength of their numbers, especially from a college rumored to be losing interest in the cause. At least one of the war correspondents swore that the Vassar students were more excited for the coming of Rosalie's army than they had been for the previous year's graduation!

Rosalie marveled at the diversity of the troops now advancing on their destination. They ranged from Vassar students to factory workers to what one of the war correspondents described as a "fair portion of the female population" all duly resolved to capture Poughkeepsie.[12] True, the Vassar girls kept mostly to themselves, and occasionally looked down their noses at the factory women, and yet these young ladies, from such different walks of life, had come to walk the suffrage walk together.

Class divisions, Rosalie warned them, would have to be overcome if ever American women wanted to win the equal rights they so richly deserved. Thus far along their route the pilgrims had seen class divisions again and again thwarting greater unity among their gender. "Mrs. So and So would speak up and declare that Mrs. Somebody else was not in her [social] set," one newspaperman covering the march had put it, "and therefore she couldn't associate with her."

Vassar College professor Laura J. Wylie and still more Vassar students met Rosalie's army of students and female factory workers as they marched into a city bedecked for their arrival as if readying itself for a gala. Yellow and black suffrage banners fluttered in the breeze. Signs reading "Votes for Women" hung everywhere. Into this festive scene strode Poughkeepsie mayor Sague. A Democrat, the mayor admitted that he himself had been an Anti not so many years ago. Now he wholly subscribed to the suffrage cause, using the logic of most astute politicians: If ya can't beat 'em, join 'em. "You would never have aroused such enthusiasm nor had the chance to speak in the places you have if you had adopted the more conventional methods of delivering your message," the mayor reminded them by way of affirmation. He, like Rosalie, believed an on-foot pilgrimage to the capital would make a powerful statement that a train ride could not.

"In the throes of a bitter debate," wrote one of the war correspondents marching with the army into Poughkeepsie, "the city [is] keyed up as it hasn't been in a mighty long time."[13] General Jones fanned the flames still further, challenging the town's anti-suffragists, including especially Professor Chamberlain, to a debate in the college auditorium that very evening. They would tell him, right to his face, and in front of the entire student body, "why a woman is jut as well able to go to the polls as she is able to bend over the washtub and bring up babies." And yet for all his hot air and antisuffragist rhetoric, Professor Chamberlain never showed his face to espouse his anti-woman venom.

Antis were often like that; they huffed and puffed and talked a good game, but when it came down to defending their dubious views in a public forum, most preferred to slink away into the night. Still, Ida and Jessie were mightily disappointed that they could not "do him up" on stage.[14]

As night descended a gentle snow begin to fall, and Rosalie, ever the general, began to make contingency plans for the next day's eighteen-mile hike to Rhinebeck. If it snowed heavily, they would have to stop short of their goal, and a delay might well jeopardize their mission. General Jones desperately wanted her troops to reach the town of Hudson by Christmas Eve so that they might spend the holiday in a brief respite of merriment and thanks. A charity ball had been scheduled for Hudson for Christmas night, and it would be a true shame to miss an affair planned so well in advance.

Snow, too, might scare away their most recent recruit, a pretty young woman and Vassar student named Miss Gladys Coursen, whom the Poughkeepsie suffrage branch had nominated to walk the rest of the way to Albany with the pilgrims. Could an eighteen-year-old handle tromping through the snow? Would she stay with the hike when the rest of her friends were home trying on their Christmas dresses? Gladys had vowed to the press that she would "stick it through until the… Capitol is reached," leaving Rosalie to hope that the girl's gumption matched her rhetoric.[15]

✿   ✿   ✿

There was something about Gladys Coursen that hadn't quite matured yet. She was too valuable a recruit, however, for the General to reject without cause. With Jessie traveling back and forth to New York City to represent their cause there, the army badly needed a solid fourth member, a healthy true-believer who would be with them all the way. And though Rosalie hated to admit it, Gladys's good looks would surely be an attraction to the war correspondents and an incentive to continue their newspaper coverage, should their interest in the three regular army officers grow stale. Perhaps the deciding factor in Rosalie's invitation to march, however, was this: Gladys Coursen could play the fiddle![16] In any event, the war correspondents had already assigned her the rank of "Corporal" and embraced her in full; but then again they had also accepted Mrs. Inez Craven into the fold, and she had disappeared shortly thereafter.[17]

One of the constant joys of the suffrage hike to date had been the fellowship the pilgrims enjoyed in the evenings, after the reporters had gone to the nearest tavern or hotel lobby to file their stories. The pilgrims made a point of bunking in adjoining quarters — for safety, for support, for the exchange of those small bits of crucial information and last-minute strategy that had to be improvised on-site. In their way these nightly meetings were not unlike the overnights they had relished as girls, only this time there was nothing frivolous or childlike about their sleepovers. Their hike to the capital was pure adventure and serious business all at once.

One of the suffragettes' favorite ways to pass the evening hours together was to read the sometimes-sensationalized newspaper accounts the correspondents had cobbled together about that day's march. Rosalie's group read the stories not for the information they contained; the pilgrims, of course, knew exactly what they had done, and not done, on any given day's journey. Instead, they read the articles for the sheer comedy they unfailingly produced. The troops certainly needed something lighthearted they could share after days in which they had

Jessie Hardy Stubbs

hiked sixteen, eighteen, sometimes even twenty-plus miles. And the newspaper accounts were so thoroughly rife with errors that they were comical; maddening, yes, but often humorously so.

Jessie, as the pilgrims' official war correspondent, was unaffiliated with any one newspaper and busy enough on the march or at the speaker's podium that she seldom had time to file any kind of proper story herself. Besides, the male newspaper editors in the city typically dismissed any article Jessie wrote as biased, predisposed, sentimental, or unprofessional — words men often directed at articles written by women about "women's issues." Still, Jessie was a writer, a journalist and provocateur through and through, and though she lacked the ample time and audience of "real" correspondents, she made for most expert company when it came to critiquing and cutting up about the sensationalized "yellow" journalism the big-city reporters often produced.

So as light snow dusted the windowsills and roofs of the modest homes of Poughkeepsie, Jessie took out her ink pen. She had resolved to write a "Letter from the Front" for *Woman's Journal* — a rare kind of magazine in Boston edited by women, for women. Her dispatch from the front would be, she assured her fellow suffragettes, without the sensationalism, exaggeration, sentimentality, and sexism of the work published by the more mainstream scribblers. Jessie would write her piece from an insider's perspective, not as a yellow journalist anxious to please his or her male editor with news sure to titillate or provoke to anger.

Safely tucked away with her suffrage sisters in the Nelson House Hotel, Jessie readied her pen and began composing.[18] She datelined her missive December 28, Poughkeepsie, NY, and began:

> To get these fountain pens rocking and keep them in perpetual motion has been the effort of the little band of pilgrims now making history in this already historic Hudson County. So constant and speedy and steady is the flow from the versatile pens of our army of special correspondents now at the front, that it is scarcely necessary for the official war correspondent of the marching body to write one line for publication. The lines *she* writes are safely locked in the hearts of managing and city editors, the result of which no man knoweth. We still have with us a representative from every powerful journal in New York....
>
> The modern newspaper reporter is a fine fiction artist who is paid for working his or her risibles. The better they do it the higher the pay! I only wish the men and women now covering the pilgrimage were getting a Mark Twain word-note. At the stopping places when the weary pilgrims get settled in adjoining rooms they nearly always get together to read the stories and make their clippings. [This] war correspondent also scans carefully the editorial page, and has been rewarded three times already. Some one of the pilgrims usually reads aloud, and we laugh until we cry over them!

Colonel Craft almost had a stroke trying to read Percy Soule's story in the *New York Times* not an hour ago. The General and [this] war correspondent were the audience and between the story itself and the… movements of its reader, both were temporarily incapacitated for further business. Enough said. There are a thousand details to look after now, and since the line will form at 9 a.m. to-morrow and move on to Rhinebeck, eighteen miles away, our friends over the world who read these lines will forgive me if I do not say more at this time, but promise it will be continued in our next, or they might better still learn with the other lay folks the new Pilgrim cry:

> Rah, rah, rah, who are we?
> We are the Pilgrims,
> Don't you see!
>
> What are we doing?
> Don't ask us.
> Buy any paper,
> They make the Fuss.

Satisfied, Jessie signed her letter "Jessie Hardy Stubbs, War Correspondent at the front — marching with General Rosalie Gardiner Jones to a peaceful capture of the Governor of New York State."

CHAPTER 7:
LIVES OF THE
RICH AND FAMOUS

The snow that had fallen overnight in Poughkeepsie had begun to pile up by morning, but General Rosalie Jones would not let it become a hindrance. Snow be damned, the much-anticipated march to Rhinebeck was on!

Just as the pilgrims' arrival into each and every town had become a spectacle — met with song and dance, babies and buntings, keys to the city and celebratory toasts, laudings and hecklings — so, too, had their departures. Sometimes Rosalie fancied her group of stalwart suffragettes could do with less fanfare. The General was not a social butterfly, like Jessie or even Ida could be on occasion; instead, she was someone for whom being on the podium or pedestal represented a hard-won victory over her own natural instinct to let others do the speaking. She imagined many leaders in history had been exactly the same way — reluctant heroes who forced themselves into the limelight for a cause greater than their own need for solitude. Certainly, America's most famous general, George Washington, had been one of these. For so many years he'd badly wanted to return to the quiet life of the Virginia gentleman farmer, but his country had needed him, and needed him badly enough that he had had to forego his most fervent personal wishes.

Rosalie's ailing feet were giving her trouble again this morning, but she had received news good enough to make her forget her pains, if only for a moment. A letter had arrived all the way from Little Rock, Arkansas! The Progressive Party there had been so moved by news of the suffrage hike that they had sent a note of congratulations from twelve hundred miles away. Rosalie sometimes forgot how quickly news of her army's historic journey had traveled; newspapers from as far away as Canada had published stories about them. After a week on the road, their march was now truly a national event, the reporters assured her, for the entire continent still looked to New York as a harbinger of things to come, a bellwether and an example to the rest of the nation. If New York saw fit to grant its women the vote, the less populous parts of the country might be expected to do the same, given that they looked to the great metropolis on the Hudson River for guidance in everything from literature to fashion.

As they stood out front of the Nelson House Hotel ready to march, they heard a voice yell, "What do you think you are doing?"[1] Rosalie spun around to locate the source of the vitriol, an angry young woman staring daggers at the suffrage General.

Rosalie looked her detractor squarely in the eye. "We are trying to help your future," she said simply, and turned around to applause from the votes-for-women crowd that had gathered. General Jones then gave the order to march, as she did each and every morning, and off they went — five strong now, with the addition of Gladys — in the direction of Rhinebeck some eighteen miles distant.

Already, though, their new recruit had given the General some cause for concern. Gladys's suffrage league had voted her as its representative to tramp to the capital, but then along had come Mr. Pelton Cannon, a man in his early thirties and a banker on the rise in Poughkeepsie. When he, in the company of Gladys's mother, had briefly joined the march, it had seemed their presence might be attributed to their support of young Gladys. Instead, Mr. Cannon, wearing his black mustache and his expensive black broadcloth coat with its lamb's wool collar, appeared bent on playing spoiler.[2] The young men of the Hudson Valley behaved like bees swarming around Gladys, and Mr. Cannon was currently doing quite a lot of buzzing, or at least it seemed. And yet he clearly wasn't the only bee in Gladys's bonnet. Mr. Griffith Bonner, or "Griff" as he was better known, had also apparently become a willing conscript in Gladys's own sizable army of admirers. For years, the reporters gossiped, Griff Bonner had begged Miss Coursen to become his wife.[3] When she became interested in the suffrage movement, he organized a Men's League for Equal Suffrage to support the cause. When she decided to march with the suffrage army, he pledged to march with her. When they had started from Poughkeepsie, however, Pelton Cannon, not Griffith Bonner, had walked on the other side of Gladys, trying his best to dissuade her from making the march.

Gladys, though, had lately taken to wearing Griff's fraternity pin as prominently as her votes-for-women badge. "The Millionaire Reporter of Poughkeepsie," as the press called the rather dashing, ginger-haired Mr. Bonner, apparently had much to recommend him. In addition to being a former Princeton man and a champion golfer, he was also a skillful writer.[4] But that wasn't all Griff Bonner was, not by a long shot. Though he was not all that much older than the fresh-faced Gladys, the press had discovered that the charming and quite rich Griff had been previously married to a showgirl starring in a London musical. The then college-aged Griff had met his youthful chorus girl crush aboard a transatlantic ocean liner, fallen madly in love with her, and married shortly thereafter, only to find his darling bride divorcing him the following year. Still, the excitable Mr. Bonner seemed to have grown up a good deal since the unraveling of that first marriage, and his and Gladys's respective fathers had been good friends for over forty years. Gladys appeared to light up whenever Griff came near, so perhaps it would be a good match after all — provided Gladys decided against Mr. Pelton Cannon.

Pelton Cannon walked with Rosalie's army for nearly two miles, ostensibly with the purpose of convincing Miss Coursen to give up the march and return to town with him to engage in what he called her "social obligations."[5] It was difficult, even under the best of circumstances, to resist the will of a man such as Mr. Cannon, who seemed to have the right sort of pedigree — employee of the Merchant Bank, member of the tennis club and country club, the Young Men's Christian Association, the Rotary Club, and so on.[6] Gladys needed the confidence now to know her own mind, and she needed her sorority, her sisterhood, to remind her of her innate good sense. So the General called a Council of War on her behalf, right there on the side of the road, while Mr. Cannon and Gladys's mother looked on impatiently, eager to return to town with their girl.

It was clear to Rosalie, Ida, Lavinia, and Jessie that Gladys desperately wanted to continue the march. So, with her sisterhood of traveling suffragettes firmly behind her, Miss Coursen sent Mr. Cannon back to town to fulfill his own "social obligations," thank you very much.

Still, it struck Rosalie as peculiar that a man of Mr. Cannon's stature could be so readily refused by so young a thing as Gladys Coursen. Could it be that Gladys considered Griff her man in the wings?

It was not Rosalie's habit to call the march to a stop, but she did so again later that morning when her corps hiked alongside the state mental asylum. Rosalie noticed a well-dressed man leaning over a stone wall, regarding the women's army with a somewhat wayward stare.

"Votes for women!" Ida declared in a voice loud enough to make the man jump.[7] "Do you believe in the right of women to vote?" she pressed.

The man continued to stare — somewhat blankly, Rosalie thought. His silence only added to the Colonel's resolve to convert him and prompted Ida to launch into a five-minute lecture on the many and necessary virtues of equality for women.

Toward the end of this long-winded speech, the man's face appeared to brighten. Resting his elbows on the wall again, he leaned over confidentially, and, looking directly at Rosalie rather than at Ida, asked, "Say, can you wiggle your ears?"

Involuntarily, Rosalie stepped back, so swiftly, in fact, that Gladys, nosing up behind the General to get a better look at the peculiar fellow, nearly fell into a ditch.

The General had prepared herself for many battle contingencies, but not for this. "Sir, I am Queen Elizabeth," she said, playing along. She then sashayed down the road, regally of course, as the rest of the pilgrims followed like a retinue.

"Hey, Your Majesty," the man called after her, "come on in. We have three Queens inside already."

The reporters were quite amused by this accidental encounter between the General and a supposed madman. Out of the corner of her eye Rosalie could see them laughing amongst themselves as they scribbled in their notebooks. That the General had played the delicate situation expertly was the consensus.

Here, on the way to Rhinebeck, the land grew considerably more rural. Food was hard to come by, and water would no longer come via waiters at hotels and quaint roadside inns, as it had further south,

Women suffrage hikers (L to R) Jessie Hardy Stubbs, "General" Rosalie Jones, and Colonel Ida Craft, who is wearing a bag labeled "Votes for Women Pilgrim Leaflets" and carrying a banner with a notice for a "Woman Suffrage Party Mass Meeting"

toward the city, but from moss-covered buckets such as the one seven-year-old Lester Crispell provided the hikers at the Colonel Archibald Rogers estate. Rogers had grown his fortunes as an official at Standard Oil, and his family home, Crumwold, was yet another of the fabulous mansions of the Hudson River Valley — though in fact it was more of a seventy-room castle in gray granite than a traditional house.[8]

Further up the road they encountered another obstruction. It wasn't Dr. O'Connor come to kidnap the General again, thank goodness, but a creature equally determined if not obstinate. Ahead of the pilgrims, smack dab in the middle of the road, stood a cow. Rosalie feared cows.

The minute Ida saw it lowing, she commenced to do what any battle-tested second-in-command would do: attempt to save her general. She leapt before the beast and attempted to shoo it away with considerable flailing of arms and the sounding of low ominous tones. The cow, of course, was having none of it. It appeared insulted, in fact, by the ridiculousness of the Colonel's efforts. Rosalie ordered a hasty retreat that sent the pilgrims behind trees to wait for the intransigent bovine to move of its own accord. The strategy worked, much to the amusement of Percy Soule from the *Times*, who joked that Rosalie's army had been "routed" by a farm animal where snow, ice, wind, and angry men had not succeeded in stopping them thus far.

Here in the thick woods and rolling hills of the Hudson Valley the original settlers had had little choice but to build their schools and churches and other public buildings on the few good roads that traversed the rugged terrain. Thus the pilgrims typically encountered several country schoolhouses a day along their route as well as many pretty little churches. Today, the first Sunday of their hike, they encountered a church with Sabbath services already in progress. Rosalie shot a look at Ida as if to say, *Don't you dare go bothering these good church-going folks with your circulars.* As it turned out, the first volley came not from Ida but from the church grounds themselves, where an elderly woman wearing an old-fashioned hat stood eyeing them critically.

"What do mean by marching on a Sunday?" she asked disapprovingly.[9]

Rosalie was readying her reply when Lavinia, already one step ahead of her general, offered her own rejoinder. "The Lord walked and talked and picked corn on the Sabbath," she pointed out.

"You're all trash — white trash," the angry parishioner fired back, and that was that. She had pronounced suffragists liable to go straight to hell for doing exactly what Christ might have done in their shoes — publicly resist an injustice that could no longer be abided. The encounter left a sour taste in the pilgrims' mouths, though the lingering negative effects were soon lifted by the sight of two young girls, nine-year-old Elizabeth and her little sister Esther, dressed in white and wearing matching large white bows in their hair. The girls presented Rosalie's army with a bundle of holly that their mother had sent the suffragettes for good luck.

The marchers had now reached Hyde Park, and at least a small part of Rosalie hoped the rich and famous of that prestigious town on the banks of the Hudson River would turn out to see her proud, if small, army pass by. Shortly thereafter the journalists began to point and speak in excited whispers. Rosalie heard the names "Astor" and "Vanderbilt" tossed about, and followed their excited gesturing toward what at a distance appeared to be an exceedingly handsome young man, an older woman, and a truly beautiful young socialite riding together in a rather extravagant car. The voices on the wind filled in the details. "Mrs. Frederick Vanderbilt, Mr. Vincent Astor, and Miss Huntington." Rosalie felt her breath catch. Word had it the three of them had motored in especially to see Rosalie and her army!

Mrs. Frederick Vanderbilt — oh, how it infuriated suffragettes when a wife was referred to only by her husband's name, as if she did not have a first name of her own! — exited the back seat of the car and walked directly to the side of the road to shake hands with the famous pilgrims. Rosalie felt drawn to Louise Vanderbilt. Here was an independent woman, a woman who had divorced her first husband to marry secretly the love of her life, Frederick. She was twelve years older than Frederick, and this, too, may have appealed to Rosalie's sense of fairness. Why was it that wealthy men seemed always to be marrying girls half their age while it was still considered scandalous for a woman such as Louise to marry a younger beau? Louise Vanderbilt had had the courage to pursue her one true love, and now here she was giving the pilgrims hearty handshakes and congratulations. It was almost too wonderful to believe.

Mr. Vincent Astor remained seated in the front seat of the car, alongside Miss Helen Huntington. Mr. Astor possessed a long nose, full lips, and dark eyes and eyebrows that seemed to smolder. He looked strong but not unkind. Rosalie wasn't the type to be impressed by appearances, but these were beautiful people! She watched half in horror and half in amusement as Colonel Craft raced to the side of Mr. Astor's car and attempted to hand her literature to Miss Huntington, who looked at first as if she had been handed a skunk!

"Well," Miss Huntington managed, "I am interested in the movement, but I don't know much about it."[10]

The Colonel was undaunted. "Will you take a circular?"

"Yes," Miss Huntington replied with what seemed a slight reluctance. Ida had achieved her objective, and looked pleased with herself. Rosalie was disappointed to learn that Vincent Astor was not at all interested in receiving one of Ida's leaflets, but then again, so few men were. Perhaps in a year or two he would feel differently.

It had been scarcely six months ago that his father, John Jacob Astor IV, the multimillionaire who had built the wonderful Waldorf-Astoria Hotel that Rosalie and her family had visited in New York City, had tragically lost his life aboard the doomed *Titanic*.[11]

What must it be like to lose your father at such a young age, Rosalie wondered, shuddering inwardly at the memory of the ocean liner that had been carrying well over two thousand passengers when it struck an iceberg in the North Atlantic. Some fifteen hundred brave souls had gone down with the ship, forcing Vincent, at a mere twenty years of age, to drop out of Harvard. The *New York Times* had called Vincent "the richest boy in the world" when he had inherited his father's fortune, nearly $70 million.[12] The lovely young woman in the front seat with him now, Miss Helen Huntington, looked to be the apple of his eye, and Rosalie couldn't help but wonder if she might quite soon carry the title so many New York debutantes appeared ready to give their right arm for: *Mrs. Vincent Astor*. And if she did, would she be all too willing to forfeit her own name in the process?

As flattered as Rosalie was to learn that she and her army were sufficiently famous to bring out the Astors and Vanderbilts of the world, the pilgrims had not been the sole reason for the celebrity appearance. The Vanderbilt mansion was but a mile from here, and Ferncliff, the Astor's 2,800-acre estate along the Hudson River, stood just beyond the city limits of Rhinebeck. Ferncliff was said to house the first indoor residential swimming pool in America, not to mention an indoor tennis court, bowling alley, and shooting range.[13] It was a wonder the Astors ever left the house at all, and to imagine that Ferncliff was only their country home! With all that opulence at his fingertips, Rosalie hoped young Vincent would use his wealth wisely.

Percy Soule, the *Times* correspondent, reckoned that the whole village of Hyde Park had turned out for the pilgrims, including the mayor and the assistant fire chief, who lent their support.[14] Was it something in the very water in Hyde Park that seemed to draw such civic-minded and patriotic people? Another native son, a young upstart New York state senator named Franklin Delano Roosevelt, had been born here at his own family's country manse. Franklin and his wife Eleanor had just engineered his re-election to a second term in the statehouse even as they dared expose the wrongdoings and greed of Tammany Hall, which was said to be the most powerful, most corrupt political machine of them all.

Hyde Park did not represent New York, though, any more than Versailles represented the whole of France, and while Rosalie may have wished that everyone might be as well-educated and civic-minded as the progressive citizens here, what good would her suffrage hike be if they were? Rosalie's army was not as much needed here as it was in the smaller towns where the old ways prevailed and where news of the social revolutions happening elsewhere in the country would be slower to take hold.

Staatsburg, the next hamlet on their march to Rhinebeck, reminded the pilgrims that a village didn't have to claim Vanderbilts and Astors and Roosevelts as its own to be open to new ways of thinking. The little town existed as no more than a dot on the map, but it seemed as though the whole of it had turned out for the arrival of the marching suffragettes — and in a festive mood as well. The general store had been decorated especially for the army, and the people there wanted a speech; Rosalie obliged. She considered aloud briefly what would reach them before she landed on her theme for the day: If physical strength was the only job requirement to be president, as so many of the Antis who wanted only male politicians seemed to think, then surely boxer Jack Johnson would have beat out Woodrow Wilson, a college professor, for the presidency! The citizens of Rhinebeck laughed at that. Jack Johnson was a heavyweight champion of the world, and while he dominated his opponents in the ring, it was laughable to think that he would be qualified to be president. Perhaps leadership didn't require physical strength after all.

Rosalie had made her very serious point with a bit of comedy, and it had worked! It was hard to make light of things that you cared about so dearly, but sometimes, the General was learning, people were willing to take you, and your cause, a bit more seriously if you showed you didn't take yourself too seriously. It was a strange paradox.

The approach to Rhinebeck lifted General Jones's spirits still further. The road canted downhill to the lovely little crossroads town where, once again, it seemed everyone must have eaten their dinner early or abandoned it altogether to witness her army's historic advance. Rosalie's troops would surely sleep well tonight in the welcoming Rhinebeck House, a hotel said to be the oldest in the country. It was built in 1709, before the revolution known as America was even a glimmer in a colonist's eye. Another general — this one by the name of George Washington — had once laid his weary head here, too.

And if even a ghost of his greatness lingered between these stout and solid walls, Rosalie and her army were sure to leave inspired.

CHAPTER 8:
A PILGRIM'S CHRISTMAS

Thus far on their journey the suffragettes had rubbed shoulders with Vanderbilts and Astors, and now, three more Rockefellers stood before them!

Lillian Dubois Rockefeller, her sister Julia, and Alethe Hosapple, their cousin, had joined the march — despite the risk of alienating their powerful parents. Lillian Rockefeller had originally promised to hike with the pilgrims all the way from New York City, but her father had strictly forbade it.[1] It was one thing to shame yourself by marching for suffrage, many of the elite Antis claimed, but quite another to shame your entire family.

Rosalie knew something of how the Rockefeller girls must feel, for Percy Soule of the *Times* had recently informed her (and the population at large) that upon receiving her daughter's war dispatch, Rosalie's mother, Mary Jones, had threatened to overtake the pilgrims by private car and drag Rosalie home. "Mrs. Jones," the *Times* had reported, "is coming from the city in a high-powered car on Sunday, and, barring tire or engine trouble, she will overtake the pilgrims."[2]

Secretly, Rosalie had been glad to wake up to snow that morning. It would mean a hard, wet hike to Hudson, if indeed they could even make it that far, but the inclement weather would also mean that her mother would be delayed as well — delayed or even possibly dissuaded entirely, given the holiday. If only the General could somehow make it to Hudson by this evening, Christmas Eve, the chances of her mother successfully apprehending her would grow to almost nil, as Mary Jones would be expected home on Christmas to perform the role of gracious hostess.

Yesterday's short slog to the village of Red Hook, day eight of their hike, had been a mixed bag. On the bright side, the day had blessed the pilgrims with many goodnesses: a greenhouse owner gifting them with a bouquet of fresh violets; the owner of the Baker Chocolate factory honoring them with an affirmative toot of the factory whistle as they passed; the employees of the Hoffman Tobacco Factory crowding the balconies to cheer them, even though none of the suffragettes smoked (but for Inez Craven, that is!).[3] Private Alice Clark had rejoined them as promised and just in time. Alice, an experienced rural hiker, had prevented the General's unwitting invitation to chemical warfare. From a distance Rosalie had mistaken a skunk for a "pretty kitty" and had made a beeline for it before being intercepted by Alice, who had saved the General from her ignorance.

Comically, Lavinia had begun calling her own aching feet her "horses," stopping at intervals to calm those balky "horses" with foot cream. For her part, Rosalie doubted whether she could have made it at all on her own badly aching feet had it not been for Alice, who provided a shoulder for her to lean on. Meanwhile, Alphonse, the loyal pilot of the army's commissary wagon, had his own problems. Upon seeing him in his furry coat and heavily laden supply car, the children of Red Hook had called out, "It's Santa Claus," and "Don't forget us! We live two houses below." As good a man as Alphonse was, he had begun giving the children who'd confused him with Old St. Nick money right from his very own pocket while reassuring them that he would indeed never forget them.

However, some of the children in Red Hook had been more naughty than nice. One boy in particular had irritated Lavinia so much that Rosalie and Ida had had to restrain the morally outraged Surgeon General; a farmer boy who crossed their path had beaten his dog right there in the road, and Lavinia would have none of it and stepped in. One could learn a lot about a person, or a society, by the way they treated women and the respect, or lack thereof, with which they treated their animals. Here was a boy, at least in Lavinia's eyes, who needed a good stern talking-to.

The fortunes of the faithful pilgrims had improved when two women suffragists met them in a horse-drawn carriage at the edge of town and escorted them into the village (though naturally Rosalie and her marchers refused a ride, as always!), only to learn that the Upper Red Hook hotel had but one bed available — one that simply had to be refused on the grounds that no self-respecting general could, in good conscience, sleep in a bed while her army slept on the cold, hard ground. Finally, in a last-minute stroke of good fortune, Mrs. Hamm, the wife of the local grocer, had appeared and agreed to feed and shelter the weary troops for the night. "The more they walk, the better they get," the kindly reporter from the *Chicago Daily Tribune* had written of the army, and while Rosalie might not always have concurred with that judgment, it seemed apt on this occasion at least.[4] In any case the General and her cohort had now trudged 111 miles from New York City in eight days.[5]

Now, by light of morning and with speed firmly in mind, Rosalie raided the general store at Upper Red Hook looking for footwear that would put them in good stead for the day's slippery hike to Hudson. The Red Hook general store offered a much smaller selection than the department stores of Madison Avenue, but Rosalie could not afford to be picky. She bought two pairs of furry "arctic" boots, four pairs of galoshes, six pairs of warm wool socks, six pairs of red mittens, four wool caps with flaps that came down over the ears, and two mufflers, for tomorrow was Christmas and her troops had worn through nearly all of their original gear.[6] Aside from the locals who walked a mile or two in celebration with the pilgrims, Rosalie's army now totaled seven inclusive of the "high command"—Rosalie, Ida, and Lavinia—along with Gladys, Katherine, Alice, and Jessie.

Rosalie departed the store with an armful of gifts for her troops and a pair of black rubber boots for herself, size eight, padded with cotton.[7] She would put on a pair of the new warm wool socks and hike them up until they could be seen above her boot tops; who cared how silly she looked so long as her feet were cozy! The reporter from the *Chicago Tribune* had figured today's hike to Hudson in ankle-deep snow as the longest yet. At twenty-four miles including detours it measured nearly twice as long as Paul Revere's historic ride from Boston to Lexington!

By just before 1:00 p.m. the suffrage pilgrims, with the three Rockefeller women in tow, had reached the little enclave of Blue Store, roughly ten miles from Red Hook, and found there the family car waiting to take the Rockefellers home. They had had their fun, and besides, this was a sensitive time to be a Rockefeller. Not only was the hardened criminal Chester "Kid" Yates still on the lam from Sing-Sing prison, but it was speculated that William Rockefeller, John D. Rockefeller's brother, had disappeared into these very woods as he attempted to evade the summons of the Sergeant-at-Arms of the United States House of Representatives.[8] Rockefeller's personal lawyer had claimed his client had been incapacitated by a mysterious illness that prevented him from testifying on possible dirty dealings at one of Rockefeller's copper mines out West. The lawyer further claimed that he had absolutely no idea where his famous client might have disappeared to; William Rockefeller was known in Tarrytown and throughout New York as a master of evasion, such that "when he goes out he is so well disguised only those who know him can recognize him."

Rumors abounded in New York City as to William's whereabouts. Some said he had sneaked out of the country to avoid testifying before Congress; others claimed that he was being sheltered by the staff of his New York City residence. However, most believed that Rockefeller had fled into the Adirondacks. Rosalie sometimes wondered which of the two fugitives would run across their rural route first.

In an odd way, she felt kindred to these two men; like her, they were both were on the run — Yates from state and federal officials, Rockefeller from the Sergeant-at-Arms and a possible congressional subpoena. Like Rosalie, they existed on the margins of society, each in their own different way. In any event Rosalie could understand why the Rockefeller women might want to keep a low profile, and she thought it sporting of them to have marched in the first place.

The afternoon dragged on, and the snow continued to fall, growing heavier and wetter as they went. At each milestone they reached, the marchers cheered, and four or five times they attempted to buoy their spirits with marching songs. Alice's favorite ditty went like this:

> I am a pilgrim
> I am a stranger
> I can tarry but a night.[9]

Automobile decorated for a woman's suffrage parade

In the pilgrims' case the lyrics were true; there was no time to tarry. At the little town of Clermont a crowd had gathered to see the snow-covered, mud-splattered suffragettes. When the crowd spotted the army, they called for a speech — but Rosalie was forced to decline; she was dog tired and the weather was worsening by the minute. Ida, however, did her best to relieve her general, summoning an impromptu speech for the cause (beside a horse trough of all things!). Rosalie's irrepressible friend hastened her delivery before rejoining her sisters to plod onward, heads down, into the deepening snow.

Before them now the road to Hudson blurred in their field of vision. Wind-driven snow clung heavily to pine boughs in a scene that, had it not threatened the army's advance, would surely have mesmerized them with its chilly beauty. Blizzard conditions greeted them when, at last, they trudged their way up Hudson's darkened main street at 6:30

p.m.[10] The General felt her legs grow weak, and an instant later she fell on the snow-covered road.[11] Ida and Lavinia rushed to her aid, and despite Rosalie's protestations, they insisted on helping her up the steps into the Worth Hotel. Once there, supporters pleaded with the General to deliver one of her highly sought-after speeches, though she feared herself too weak in the knees to deliver. But if Colonel Teddy Roosevelt could finish his speech with a would-be assassin's bullet lodged in his chest, then she could give a speech that "set the rafters ringing" — and she did.[12] Rosalie Jones and Theodore Roosevelt where both Long Islanders, and Long Islanders were a tough breed indeed!

After they had checked in to their rooms the women immediately stepped out of their damp clothes and wrapped themselves in warm blankets to stave off chills. All day long they had marched directly into the face of a driving snow, to the point that ice crystals had formed on their eyelashes. The women of Rosalie's army looked more like creatures born of some strange frozen planet than they did like ladies who would, in less than twenty-four hours, dazzle at a charity ball.

"Those who wish may go to supper," Rosalie declared, "but I am going to bed."

The hotel staff informed Rosalie that a letter was waiting for her. She opened it with trepidation, fearing the worst: another threatening communiqué from her mother, who had no doubt grown more concerned with the return of Dr. O'Connor from Wappingers Falls without her beloved daughter. Since then the headlines had been dominated by a completely new kind of criminal ruthless enough to add to her mother's long list of worries — auto bandits.[13] Three days earlier in Rosalie's New York City, thugs had attacked two innocent clerks from a silk company, beaten them to unconsciousness, and robbed them of over $1,000 before escaping in a high-powered car. Such news would no doubt be used to further discourage young women and girls from leaving their homes at night, let alone walking 175 miles through the remote countryside!

Instead of an irate note from her mother, however, the General was pleased to find in the envelope an original poem titled "The Night Before Christmas," written by Elizabeth Aldrich of New York City. One of Rosalie's favorite verses read:

For there to my wondering eyes did appear,
The miniature army of four tired dears,
With an odd draggled General, weary of bones,
I knew in a moment twas Rosalie Jones.[14]

Rosalie read the lyrics again and again, letting the words warm her, until they, like the light itself, begin to flicker and grow dim, and before long she was fast asleep.

☼ ☼ ☼

Christmas, at long last!

Rosalie sipped on a cup of tea so hot it burned her lips as she spread the copy of the *New York Times* across her lap. Yesterday, H. Percy Soule of that newspaper had invited her to write a Christmas dispatch to the suffrage faithful back home, and she had been happy to oblige. Now here it was, a black-and-white Christmas greeting on newsprint.

Merry Xmas from the Marchers
by Rosalie Gardner Jones
General of the Suffrage Army
by telegram to the editor of *The Times*

> The suffrage pilgrims in the march to Albany, through the *Times*, wish those who are fighting for the cause a very merry Christmas…. We know that some good has been accomplished by our rather spectacular march, more good results than could have been accomplished by a more sedate "calling" upon the Governor-elect….
>
> The people of this state have seen us, they have asked us questions, and we have had a chance to explain to them face-to-face just what this great cause represents. And tired as we are all after our long march, we are happy this Christmas day, and we wish the gladdest of the season's greetings to all suffragists all over the country.

Rosalie folded the paper of record up with no small amount of satisfaction, and stared out the window of her hotel room at the snowy streets of Hudson, decked out before her with boughs of holly and pine. She felt fortunate for the opportunity to write her supporters, fortunate to be out of the wind and the weather, for once near a bath, and radiant heat, and clean, dry socks. She could think of no more meaningful a Christmas than the one she was having, 125 arduous miles from hearth and home.

The General wasn't sure when in her past, exactly, she had realized that there was something wrong with the way her countrywomen and men celebrated this most sacred of holidays. Christmas, she had always been taught, was meant to be about giving, about selfless acts of service and charity, more than it was about things readily consumed and purchased. Every evening, when she and Ida, Lavinia, and sometimes Jessie gathered together to read the newspaper coverage of their march, they found oversized advertisements trumpeting "Xmas Gifts, Special Terms and Prices! Buy Now, Pay Next Year!" One had even promised "the MOST LIBERAL TERMS ever offered" — just like that, all in caps — on such luxuries as Plush and Persianna coats, fur accessories, and everything else tasteful women were purported to desire.[15] Others advertised "Diamonds on Credit… Xmas Presents!"[16]

The adverts invariably featured people dressed to the nines in the season's choicest fashions. The finely clad women in the ads might indeed have reminded Rosalie of her mother, and this in turn caused her to wonder just how happy her mother, or for that matter her father, had ever truly been, given all their worldly possessions. Her mother, for example, made a great to-do each and every Christmas, practically insisting that Rosalie and the other grown children return to the family table. But it had often seemed to Rosalie that her mother was more focused on creating a Christmas after some storybook image, or a Christmas that would look good in the eyes of others, than on honoring the true spirit of the season. Spirit was a difficult thing to bottle and sell, but one thing was sure, Rosalie's suffragettes had it in spades.

Just a few weeks before, the Women's Club of Chicago had adopted a resolution calling for a "sane Christmas." No expensive presents were to be given by any of its members unless to a needy person or a deserving child. Pearls and diamonds would be considered especially "bad form." Rosalie admired the principled stance of these women, one that had resulted in the somewhat comical headline "Santa Claus Has Ban on Diamonds."[17]

Back home in New York, a noble organization calling itself the "Do-Something Club" had run an inventory of Christmas wishes in the newspaper under the heading "The Last of the 500 Cases—Who Will Help Them?" The list, so full of destitute wives and widows and young girls, couldn't help but break the General's heart. Case number 469 read simply, "Widow; little girl, heart trouble; very small income; special food and rent." Another solemnly stated, "Two girls support old mother; mother sick; special food."[18]

In setting out on their impossible trip through snow and bitter cold, through ice and wind with little more than cold trail mix as their daily rations, Rosalie's army had come to better understand what true tribulation felt like. Her little band amounted to its own kind of do-something club, and the something it hoped to do stood to benefit all women; and this, Rosalie felt, was a gift whose joy would never grow old or out of fashion. The gift of a vote was not the same as food or daily bread, and yet women hungered for it nonetheless — and with good reason.

The marchers had lived like paupers for days on end, so today of all days the General wanted to make sure her hard-pressed troops received the care and concern they had earned for their exceptional loyalties. Certainly, she had had surprises in store for them, the first of which had been her announcement that the group would be allowed to sleep until noon today, and it was nearing noon now. They would be well rested for tonight's charity ball.

Not one in her platoon had reported homesickness so far.[19] Down the hall Rosalie could hear the sounds of her infantrywomen readying themselves for the day's events. Rosalie counted six in the corps as of this morning, inclusive of the regular army — herself, Ida, and Lavinia — along with Katherine Stiles, who had, with each passing day affiliated herself more publicly with their cause, despite her husband's important position with the Associated Press. Katherine had begun to accompany Jessie on some of her speeches, and had impressed everyone with a stirring votes-for-women speech of her own delivered at the Rhinebeck church two nights earlier. Fit as a fiddle, Private Alice always added pep to the pilgrims' steps, summoning a marching song when they needed it most. Finally, there was Gladys, who had become a regular by now; she hadn't missed a mile since joining the group in Poughkeepsie.[20]

After providing for their promised rest, General Jones checked in on each of the pilgrims in their respective rooms. She wished them each a very merry Christmas, and found that they, in turn, were ready to fight their first suffragist battle of the day — the Battle of the Ice Skating Rink! The opponents in this case were the young people of Hudson, some of whom needed some convincing. All of the troops stood ready except Lavinia, whose knees and ankles were several decades older than the others' and therefore needed more rest.

Colonel Craft was as eager as a puppy — she always came alive whenever there were potential converts to be won. She was not, however, so keen on the idea of skating with the children and teenagers of the town of Hudson. The minute Ida laced up her skates Rosalie understood why: Colonel Craft had walked nearly 125 miles on foot, but she was not exactly the best skater. By contrast, Rosalie found the sport readily came back to her after a few trips around the ice. Before she knew it, she was gliding rhythmically along, the young people of Hudson urging her on as she went.

Rosalie was wary of skating for long, however. Already she could feel the stress on her overworked ankles. Two days ago, on the hike to Red Hook, she had had to lean on her fellow officers just to continue, and no amount of holiday fun now would bring her to jeopardize the rest of the march. She stopped, skated to the center of the rink, and signaled the manager, who in turn brought all skating to a halt so that Rosalie might say few words. There in the middle of the rink Rosalie addressed more than one hundred skaters.[21] She found them interested, despite their thinking more perhaps of sugar plum fairies than of the suffragist chestnuts she might offer. Among the most avid listeners were the proud members of Hudson's own suffragist organization, who'd decided to hold their holiday meeting on ice.[22]

But who could fault the young people of Hudson if perchance they were more than usually distracted; they had come to the rink to spend this most joyous of holidays gliding on the ice, not listening to a speech on equal rights for women. Rosalie found herself a bit preoccupied as well, for she was already thinking about the surprise she had waiting for her troops back at the hotel.

When, not long after, Rosalie entered the warm hotel lobby with her troops trailing behind her, she saw immediately that her plan had been exercised perfectly in her absence. The manager of the hotel had offered up his entire office for the pilgrims' celebration and had spruced up the space with all manner of holly and Christmas greens. Bells and other ornaments hung from the high ceiling. And a magnificent Christmas tree, all agleam with candles and surrounded by presents, stood as the centerpiece. For nearly ten days Rosalie Jones had played the role of general; now she would play the role of Santa Claus. She had acquired a special gift for each member of her regular army so that when they gathered on the settee in the parlor, she had something for them as a reward for "bravery in the performance of duty."[23]

Playing Santa Claus proved much more enjoyable than playing drill sergeant or taskmaster. Still, General Jones felt even this joyous occasion required its own special decree: For the next hour at least, they must direct their thoughts to the spirit of the season and mustn't once mention the votes-for-women cause![24]

Rosalie looked on in anticipation as Colonel Craft, at the General's request, performed her best impression of a Santa's elf, distributing the gifts to each member of the small yet mighty army. A mixture of soothing lotions, cold creams, foot powders, balms, and tonics of every possible description were pulled eagerly from gift boxes; galoshes, woolen socks, earmuffs came next. Rosalie had hoped to create the perfect care package to cure what ailed her long-distance hikers.[25] And she had acquired wonderfully impractical gifts for her faithful troopers, too — candy, toy automobiles, and even a slipper for Lavinia to replace the one she had lost on the previous day's hike.

Rosalie thrilled at the almost childlike delight on her comrades' faces. They had been loyal throughout, and they deserved these small tokens of thanks and so much more. Without the abiding loyalty of Colonel Craft and Surgeon General Dock, in particular, the march surely wouldn't have lasted beyond Yonkers on that very first day, when many a suffragette (and suffragtte's dog!) had seen fit to quit. Partnering with the war correspondents who had covered the march thus far, the troops presented their general with a souvenir copy of *Pilgrim's Progress*, that great book from so many hundreds of years ago about a young person, Christian, on a spiritual journey to Mount Zion. Inside its front cover the army had inscribed to the General: "And it came to pass that when the people heard the trumpets and the people shouted, the walls of Albany fell flat."[26]

"That they will," Rosalie said quietly as she read the inscription, "and we will march around them ten times, one for each state in the union that has granted suffrage to women!"

The walls of Albany, New York — not Jericho! Her well-versed soldiers had adapted the Bible's Book of Joshua to speak to the cause of women voters. Each of the marchers had penned an additional individual inscription as well. The very first read:

> Where are you going, my pretty maid?
> I'm going a-suffering, sir, she said.
> May I go with you, my pretty maid?
> If you carry the baggage, sir, she said.[27]

And below it one of her more poetic pilgrims had penned:

> Theirs not to reason why.
> Theirs but to tramp or die.
>
> — The Noble Six Hikers

Fairly bursting now with gratitude and pride, Santa Jones had one final surprise for her good-spirited pilgrims: a luscious, beautiful chocolate cake, big enough to feed an army. Rosalie unveiled it with a grand flourish and, having acquired a knife, was bending over to slice the confection when Gladys whispered something shocking indeed in the General's ear. Rosalie could hardly believe what she had just heard. Young Gladys had just whispered news of her engagement to Griffith Bonner — the "millionaire newspaperman" from Poughkeepsie who had been marching beside her occasionally in the last few days!

The General congratulated Gladys with a joyful embrace, and urged her to share the news with the rest of the troops, which Gladys did, wearing an excited blush on her face. It was to be a "three months probation engagement," she told them, as the army gathered around in celebration.[28] After that time, if all was still well, she would formally accept Mr. Bonner's engagement.

Rosalie looked on with no small amount of pride. The probationary period had been a wise decision. Why rush into something so important as marriage?

Just like that, their Christmas cake had become an engagement cake. The happy chatter over Gladys's news stopped for a moment then, as each of the suffragettes studied her own mountain of yuletide cake in a silence near to reverence.

There followed a moment of devoted, almost sensuous consumption until three nearly simultaneous cries of surprise broke the silence of the hotel parlor. The first belonged to the now happily engaged Mr. Bonner, who held up a cake-encrusted thimble for all to see, followed shortly thereafter by one of the army privates, who had found in her slice a wedding band. The cunning Griff Bonner, or else the equally crafty Gladys Coursen, had managed to fool the General, no doubt in cooperation with the hotel baker, to sneak the wedding charms into the Christmas cake. The tradition of baking charms into the cake was as old as America itself, dating all the way back to Colonial times. The thimble was said to symbolize old age and spinsterhood, at least in French New Orleans, though it was hard for Rosalie to imagine the dashing Griffith Bonner as an old maid. Meanwhile, tradition had it that the one lucky enough to find the ring in her cake would be the very next to marry. The General was almost glad she had not found the band in her slice; she wasn't yet ready to say "I do" — and besides, she was happily married to the votes-for-women movement.

After dessert, the suffrage pilgrims offered yet another round of hearty congratulations to the young couple, and the army disbanded to prepare for its next engagement: the annual Hudson ball, the highlight of the town's social calendar. The dance was be given for the benefit of the Hudson Hospital, and its patronesses were a trio of incredible local women who had survived the sinking of the *Titanic* just six months earlier. Tonight's ball was to be a celebration of survival then, of endurance, and who better to represent those enduring virtues than Miss Cornelia Andrews, her niece Gretchen Longley, and Anna Louisa Hogeboom.

Anna had been traveling in France and Italy throughout 1911, and had booked passage back to Hudson with her sister Cornelia and her niece Gretchen. The three women had boarded the RMS *Titanic* in South Hampton as first-class passengers, and when Gretchen checked into her cabin she had found a curious little note that read:

> **G**ood weather
> **R**efreshments
> **E**very desire
> **T**ommies to burn
> **C**hocolate ice cream
> **H**eavenly evenings
> **E**ntire meals
> **N**o regrets

The note was an acrostic, the first letter of each word on the list, top to bottom, spelling out *Gretchen*. But the items listed in the poem, including "good weather," "heavenly evenings," and "no regrets" could not help but cause a chill in retrospect.[29]

As the great ship sank Gretchen and her companions had boarded Lifeboat #10 to find not a single crewman aboard, so the athletic Miss Longley had done what any brave young woman would do — she had grabbed an oar and pulled her way through the rough seas until her party could be rescued. Gretchen's life-saving heroism had made national news, and a good thing, too, thought Rosalie, for women were too often portrayed as passive, weak, and hysterical during emergencies. Gretchen Longley surely would have made a hearty suffrage pilgrim had she so chosen. General Jones would have been glad to have her among her ranks.

As the trampers gathered up their lovely Christmas presents and prepared to retire to their rooms, Rosalie delivered one more surprise to them: In her final preparations for the march she had shipped several very special trunks to Hudson, having every faith that, in spite of the odds, the pilgrims would reach there by Christmas Day. Slowly now, and with a sense of mounting drama, she revealed their contents.

Costumes!

The women of Rosalie's army could hardly believe their eyes. After countless days of wearing the same marching uniform and the few spare garments Alphonse could carry in his supply car, they couldn't help but marvel at the elaborateness of Rosalie's planning and the intricacy of the designs she unveiled.

Rosalie passed out each costume to its wearer, explaining that the army would be going to the ball costumed as spirits.

Spirits?! But what kind of spirits? the pilgrims asked.

The spirits of the great American women's rights activists of the past, the General informed them, suffragists each in their own right.[30]

Rosalie now summoned her regular army and explained the masquerades each would perform.

Jessie Hardy Stubbs, who had traveled from New York City to Hudson this very day to join her comrades for the night's charity event, would go dressed as "The Spirit of Margaret Brent of 1647," the woman who had gone before the assembly of the then-colony of Maryland to demand that she be allowed to vote, and was therefore considered "the original American suffragette."[31]

Rosalie would attend the ball dressed as Abigail Adams, the former First Lady of these United States, who had warned her husband John not to neglect provisions for the rights of women in the formation of a new American government. If he and the other Framers failed, she predicted, the women of America would one day "rise in their might." Rosalie wore a costume of pink and blue, a blue satin petticoat under a

Members of the Men's League for Woman Suffrage with others, outside the headquarters of the Woman's Suffrage Party of Manhattan

draped and swagged overskirt and looped side hoops of flowered pink silk. Her shoes were black velvet with buckles.

Colonel Ida Craft received a garnet velvet gown and a Quaker cap; she was to impersonate Lucretia Mott, the Quaker abolitionist, women's rights activist, and social reformer who had helped write the Declaration of Sentiments at the famous Seneca Falls Convention of 1848, an event thought by many to be the first-ever public women's rights meeting in the United States. The Declaration of Sentiments — a kind of Declaration of Independence for American women — had called for "the women of this country to secure to themselves the sacred right to the elective franchise." Now, almost sixty-five years after Elizabeth Cady Stanton and her mentor, Lucretia Mott, had called for votes for women, Colonel Craft was doing just that — fighting to secure a long-refused yet basic right.

Private Katherine Stiles, Rosalie announced, would stand for the Spirit of 1776, portraying in her black velvet gown and matching high heels Mercy Warren, the Revolutionary War-era author and political commentator who was one of the very first to call for the inclusion of a Bill of Rights in the Constitution, and who fought tooth and nail against the British Crown's infringements on the personal and civil liberties of the colonists.

Last but not least, Rosalie's newest member, Gladys Coursen, would attend the dance as "The Spirit of 1912." As the youngest regular private under Rosalie's command, it was only fitting that she represent the spirit of the now. Gladys, the bride-to-be, would be the only one of the troops to don a contemporary dress, and as an accessory she would wear a placard bearing the name of the states where women had earned the vote: Colorado, Utah, Idaho, Washington, California, Oregon, Kansas, Arizona, and Texas. Rosalie had planned Gladys's costume as a reminder that suffrage victories had already been won in the Great Plains and far West, and a necessary visual reminder that the vast majority of states, including all of those in the east, still denied women the right of enfranchisement.

The army looked at their costumes in wonderment, considering how they would transform themselves into these historic women — indeed, conjure their very spirits — in the mere hour or two that remained before the beginning of the ball. It would be a tall order, they claimed, as they disappeared into their rooms to make ready.

But, then again, meeting tall orders had become the specialty of Rosalie's army.

✿   ✿   ✿

The army stood before their general now in full costume. They had spent the late afternoon readying themselves for their debut, and already the suffragettes could hear the sweet strains of music coming from the dance floor. They were more than eager to join in, yet the General held them back, issuing her most peculiar directive yet: Each costumed member of the army must position herself among the evening's revelers in a prominent position, and for one full hour they mustn't move or speak while the rest of the partygoers whirled around them in yuletide merriment.[32]

Some members of the army were tempted to protest, but they held their tongues; General Jones had issued her orders. And in the 125 miles they had thus far marched at her side, she had yet to steer them wrong.

What a sight it was, the pilgrims stock-still, stone-faced in their period garb, as the merry-makers threw back their heads in laughter and clinked their glasses, carrying on the way people do at parties. Like any good general, Rosalie followed her own orders, and was glad for it. To stand unmoving in the face of so many enticements tested her army's discipline. The revelers here tonight must know that her soldiers weren't here merely to have fun but instead to stand, quite literally, for something that was centuries old — the American woman's indomitable fighting spirit. Tonight Rosalie was determined to celebrate the American woman's historic ability to look beyond immediate gratification in her pursuit of truly timeless and lasting gains.

Rosalie's plan had been formulated to encourage discussion and speculation. And as she stood wearing her blue and pink dress with its dramatic side-hooped overskirt, many of Hudson's most charitable citizens stopped before her to discuss who she was meant to represent. Rosalie and others had powdered their hair to further look the part, and still the General was surprised by how many of the attendees of the ball struggled to name her, a founding mother of their very own nation!

How easily Rosalie's foremothers had been forgotten, despite having fought many of the same battles the army was fighting today, and with equal spirit. How readily do such brave women slip into the pages of the past, forgotten and mothballed, as if each new effort to right a societal wrong had been the only such effort ever made. Often it seemed to General Jones that her countrymen and women had developed a certain amnesia about their past, but perhaps this was not a national trait so much as it was a regrettably human one.

When her army's hour as human statues was up, the General led her soldiers out of the ballroom in a silent march. Once they had exited, words and observations of all they had just seen, heard, and felt gushed from the "spirits" as each relayed her impressions. Rosalie smiled. Her rather unorthodox order had achieved the desired effect, and now the blithe spirits could return and dance like flesh-and-blood girls!

How wonderful it felt to dance again, Rosalie felt, spinning and whirling across the floor with her sister suffragettes, to drink and eat and speak of events both big and small, worldly and mundane. On the trail she had worried she might forget her feminine graces, but she was relieved now to find they came back to her quickly once conjured.

Though she was dressed as Abigail Adams, Rosalie felt a bit more like Cinderella as the clock marched on toward midnight and the dancers danced out their yuletide cheer. At last, sweetly fatigued and pleasantly drowsy, the charitable revelers moved to find their coats and head out into snow as perfect as the kind that fell in children's snow globes. Rosalie watched as Gladys, still costumed as the Spirit of 1912, left arm-in-arm with her new fiancé. Griff positively glowed, and who could blame him? Gladys Coursen, suffragette, was indeed a catch, and she had said yes — or at least yes provisionally.

And yet at that moment the irrepressible Mr. Bonner appeared more intent on a rather animated discussion he seemed to be having with Alderman McCarthy of Hudson, who returned Mr. Bonner's entreaties, whatever they might be, with a face flushed with good cheer. Rosalie surely couldn't be blamed if she kidded the ebullient Griff further as Rosalie's army and the war correspondents said their good-byes and drifted out into the glittering snow toward the warmth of the Worth Hotel. Did the millionaire reporter of Poughkeepsie have more secrets to share on this Christmas Day? Did he have still more romantic tricks up his sleeve?

Upon their return, Rosalie, her officers, Mr. Bonner, and Alderman McCarthy settled in gratefully around the Christmas tree under which, this very morning, Gladys had announced her engagement.[33] And now, true to form, Mr. Bonner was at it again, playing Cupid on another romantic errand. Rosalie could hardly believe her ears, but had not the indefatigable Griffith Bonner just offered Alderman McCarthy a handsome sum to perform the marriage ceremony right there on the spot?

And now the reporters were egging their fellow reporter on, telling Gladys that where engagements were concerned delays were dangerous and that she "might just as well have it over with." A gaggle of them had descended upon Hudson in anticipation of the drama offered by the charity ball and its aftermath, including M. N. Stiles of the Associated Press (Katherine's reporter husband); Virginia Hudson, of *New York Press*; Emma Ragbee, *New York Tribune*; Gertrude A. Marvin, *New York Sun*; Henry Parker, the *New York Journal*; J. O. Smith, *New York World*; H. Percy Soule, *New York Times*; William Conley, *New York Globe*; and Martin Casey, *Brooklyn Eagle*. And, naturally, who could forget the star reporter-of-the-hour, Griffith Bonner of the aptly named *Poughkeepsie Star*!

It was difficult for Rosalie to blame the journalists; many of them had traveled with her army for the duration of their journey, enduring some of the same privations. Still, the nerve of them! Gladys had been engaged for all of a handful of hours, and already the newshounds wanted her to get it over with in time for their morning editions!

Gladys now turned her attentions to the excitable pack of them that, like it or not, included her new fiancé, Mr. Bonner. "I am going to insist upon his telling the whole truth," she said, sending her intended a withering look that made him blush. "Did I say that I will marry you?!"

"Well, you told me that in three months, during which I would be on a sort of probationary period, that you would accept me provided I…" Mr. Bonner, duly chastened by the reprimand, attempted to slip a conciliatory arm around the waist of his fiancée, but to no avail.

"You know that I didn't say yes, and why, then, do you try to convey such an impression?" Gladys said, falling back into her chair. She declared that if the "horrid" reporters so much as dared announce her private engagement publicly, she would call the whole thing off, though Rosalie doubted very much she would stick to that pledge. Still, she admired Gladys's spunk, and one thing was certain: She had put Mr. Bonner in his place!

And now, off in the corner, Griff was doing his best to set things right with a reporter from the *New York Press*. "We are engaged," he could be overheard saying. "That is, I believe we are; but there is a slight string to it. Miss Coursen has put me on a three months' probation. She wants to be sure I will devote my entire time to her, as is natural. My social duties, of course, have made it necessary for me to have many young woman friends. But I intend to show her I can be true."[34] The *Press* reporter couldn't be blamed for any skepticism. It was well known that Bonner's "social duties" included attending dances at places with names like Sherry's and Delmonico's.

Tonight had belonged to Gladys, surely, but also to the army as a whole. And yet as wonderful and righteous as the charity dance had been, the night's festivities had been an outlier. As if to demonstrate that fact, every so often the General would catch the eye of one of her soldiers across the crowded dance floor, and an unspoken understanding would pass between them. They all knew that tomorrow they would be on the march again, that the capital and the inauguration of the new Governor lay in wait, now little more than thirty miles distant. Tomorrow they would turn from civilians and ladies back into soldiers again, and by the look on the suffragettes' faces, they were ready for that transformation.

Tonight, though, the stars were in their eyes, as outside the evening's glistening snowmelt promised fairer weather to come. Tomorrow would be a challenging, messy hike into the unknown. But with any luck, the sun would shine on Rosalie's army once again.

CHAPTER 9:
JINGLE BELLS AND SHOTGUN SHELLS

Who could rise from their bed the day after Christmas without at least a small groan of disappointment?

But this was no ordinary holiday season for Rosalie Jones and her troopers, as their true Christmas present awaited them a few more days down the road, when they would march into the capital. "The three storm stressed pilgrims have given the cause of woman suffrage a Christmas present beyond price," women's rights activist Anna Cadogan Etz wrote in *Woman's Journal*, calling Rosalie and her troops a "wonder." "That it would secure more newspaper space for a greater length of time than even the great suffrage parades, no one dreamed," she wrote.[1]

Today the fervent hope for a more equitable, more just New Year ahead stirred the pilgrims from their beds in the Worth Hotel, and with fond memories of the previous night's charity ball still warming them from within, they assembled for a snowy exit out of Hudson town. The reporters had ignored Gladys's pleas for privacy, of course, and the gossip-mongering headlines read, "Griffith Bonner Is Lover"[2] and "Impetuous Lover Rebuffed."[3]

The clock read 10:00 as Rosalie formally resumed the march with a cry of "Forward!"[4] Many of the townspeople of Hudson were still tucked away inside their warm homes — dreaming of gingerbread fairies perhaps, or the Spirits of Suffrage Past at last night's charity ball. But the children of the village were up, and the sound of their mirth filled the ears of the pilgrims as they approached the sledding hill along Fairview Avenue.

"Come and slide with us!" the children cried.

A brief look passed between the General and Ida. Should they really stop to toboggan when they had barely begun their day's march?

But they were emissaries after all — not just of serious causes and purposes, but also of joy and joy's sister: adventure.

With a running start, and lifting her staff high above her head, Rosalie launched herself onto the slide and whirled down the hill with a sense of freedom she hadn't felt for ages. Then, leaping up to dust the snow from her overcoat, she declared to the children who had gathered around her that she would quite happily take another turn, and she did! Nearly all the other marchers took a turn as well, to Rosalie's great satisfaction.

Still, their purpose was winning women's votes, and this could not be done on a sleigh or a toboggan, much as she might have wished. So Rosalie once again, and with no small measure of reluctance, gave her troops their marching orders, and forward they went onto the soggy roads in the direction of their destination of Stockport.

The beginning of each marching day held such promise for Rosalie, not to mention uncertainty. Her comrades had only to take that first step each morning to make themselves and their beliefs visible, thereby creating a cascade of effects and impacts, both seen and unseen. Rosalie quite liked the feeling of anticipation that marked the beginning of the day's hike. Her work on behalf of the votes-for-women cause had taught Rosalie that some activists were good starters and others were better finishers — and there was the intermediate period to consider as well. A true pilgrim needed to be good at all three.

It didn't take long before the day's first surprise occurred. The woods on the way to the village of Stockport were alive with shotgun blasts and explosions of all kinds. Hunting season had begun, Rosalie's army had been told, and those who weren't out stalking their prey seemed to be intent on unsettling the pilgrims, or celebrating the spirit of the season; it was often hard to determine which.

Rosalie startled to the sound of three explosions in succession from the hillside above, where the workers at the cement factory had waited for the army to come into view before setting off their ear-shattering charges. Was theirs a salute? A prank? Or an attempt to startle her soldiers as if they were just so many quail? Perhaps it was a bit of all three. Men were noisy people, and never more so, the General had noticed, than when they were forced to confront the uncomfortable. Maybe it was the boy buried inside every man — the one who dealt with ideas beyond his comprehension by producing some loud effect sure to return attention to him. In any event, the blasts from above, coupled with the sound of gunshots in the woods all around them, rattled Rosalie and her companions, who surely wouldn't be blamed if they had begun to feel more like prey than protestors.

And then there were the cars whirring by on the Albany Road. They hurried to and fro as if keeping pace with the frenetic rhythm of this busy season. A car whisked by them at such speed, in fact, that the gust from its wake stirred the strands of hair beneath their marchers' hats. The women watched as, up ahead, the car skidded to a stop and circled back. Had the driver — a man — returned to praise them, heckle them, or question them? It was nearly always one of these, but almost never any two in combination. Rosalie braced herself, as she always did when the by-now-familiar pattern presented itself.

Fortunately, the man only wanted to offer them a lift. They looked tired, he commented (true enough!). The General, however, politely declined his offer — as she had each and every time such an offer had been made previously. To accept this man's apparent charity would be to break the very pledge she had made to her supporters — the pilgrims would make the entire journey on foot, without paying a fare for any of the miles traversed.

The goal all along had been to make the march something spectacular and memorable in order to draw attention to the righteousness and importance of their cause. But little had Rosalie known what a sensation a small band of women walking — walking! — on the side of a rural road would cause. On its face, nothing could be more unremarkable, but in a world obsessed with mechanized travel, long-distance walking in remote places stood out as something only a prophet or a quack would do. Still, General Jones could imagine it no other way — what was a pilgrim but someone who made her journey humbly, and on foot?

And the people… my goodness the people! Lots of activists in places like Brooklyn and Manhattan *talked* about getting out of the city to meet with salt-of-the-earth citizens, but few actually followed through. To do so would have been to open themselves up to the unknown, or perhaps even the realization that these salts-of-the-earth weren't quite the tidy stereotypes citified New Yorkers made them out to be. Edward Sheldon and his wife were prime examples. Rosalie and her army had only just met Mr. Sheldon, who had been chopping down a tree on the side of the road that led to Stockport.

He stopped chopping to declare, quite loudly, that he was entirely for votes for women. Rosalie's army cheered him until Mrs. Sheldon returned from carrying a bundle of wood to the house. She did so wearing a distinctly disapproving look. "I don't believe in that," Mrs. Sheldon said, adding on behalf of her husband, "and he doesn't either."

Well, not even Lavinia or Ida, who always seemed to have a ready reply for the Antis, had an answer for that!

But General Jones did. As her pilgrims marched away from the Sheldons, Rosalie turned to the war correspondents and quipped, "That woman has a vote already," she said, smiling as she gestured back toward Mrs. Sheldon, who had recommenced supervising her husband's hatchet job.

The newspapers had described the five-mile hike from Hudson to Stockport as "quick" and "easy."[5] And yet wasn't everything easy to the person who didn't have to do it?! Still, General Jones appreciated the chance for a shorter day. It was not yet 1:00 p.m. and already they could see the rushing Kinderhook River, running swiftly with the day's snowmelt, and just beyond it the old general store that marked Stockport Center and their day's final destination. Though the temperatures had warmed nicely, and the day's hike been a brief one by comparison, the terrain had never been worse, and mud clung to the pilgrims' boots and oozed into their woolens. They would all be very happy at the chance for rest and relief. Lavinia, in particular, with her aching and arthritic joints, picked up her pace as the destination neared.

As they crossed the bridge over the swiftly moving waters of the Kinderhook, the General, with her watchful eye, noticed two men out in front of the general store, a single chair between them, which they appeared to have conscripted as a launch pad for some sort of rocket.

Rosalie nodded wordlessly to her companions, giving them a look that said, *Be mindful. Keep your wits about you.* After shouting "Votes for women!" Lavinia looked on as the rocket blasted off sideways and tragically off-course, veering wildly. Instead of aiming for the heavens, the firework made a beeline in her direction, and before Lavinia knew what had happened, the missile struck her squarely in the overcoat. The force of the impact knocked the staff from her hand. General Jones called a temporary halt to the hike, rushing to Lavinia's aid. It was time for her troops to return the favor to their resident nurse, for once fussing over Lavinia instead of the other way around. Thank heavens the Surgeon General was more startled than hurt.

The men came over and offered an apology, though it struck the army as unsatisfactory. Rosalie was a seasoned enough campaigner to know that mishaps like this one were bound to happen. They were the kind of "accidents" that sometimes didn't seem like accidents at all, but rather clumsy and often violent attempts at intimidation. From the raucousness of their good cheer, it was clear the citizens of Stockport wished to express enthusiastic welcome to the pilgrims, but still.

Rosalie had expected fireworks on the day's march, but not necessarily of the literal kind. And as her army settled into their encampment for the night at Sagendorph's Hotel, Lavinia's singed and dirtied coat served as a reminder that a march for equal rights did indeed take a soldier's fortitude.[6] The suffragists had now hiked a total of 130 miles from New York City.

☼   ☼   ☼

December 27th, and the world marched on as usual… but didn't it always? Newspapers brought word of increased patrols and extra guards on hand at British trains stations, as "militant" suffragettes attempted to derail trains by tampering with signal wires. In Britain and elsewhere in Europe, a woman's right to vote had become a matter of life and death.[7]

Another of the day's headlines read in big bold type: "Can't Find Rockefeller — Believe He Is Skulking in the Adirondacks."[8] And then of course lighter items decorated the pages of these same newspapers —

human interest stories the war correspondents called them — including one relaying word of eleven-year-old Grace Odell of Sterling, Illinois, reported to have been fast asleep for eighty-six hours straight! General Jones could only fantasize about what such rest must feel like. Amid all these headlines, newspapers across the nation ran a photo of a proud yet tired Rosalie Jones and Ida Craft bravely wielding their birch-bark walking sticks.

For the pilgrims, however, the real news of the day waited until that evening. A driving rain had turned to heavy snow, slowing their progress on their ten-mile trudge to the small village of Valatie. It was well after dark when finally they arrived at the Pine Bush Inn, soaked head to toe and chilled to the bone.[9] The pilgrims immediately dispersed for their rooms, and the very last thing they wished to do, when they emerged from their respective baths, was to return to the freezing night. Still, word came to them that a number of supporters had gathered at the farm home of James Valentine several miles north of town to hear Rosalie talk, and the army was resolved, despite the weather, to keep their promise.

By the time the last plate and fork had been collected, it was well past 7:00, and the roadways outside Mr. Valentine's farm home had disappeared beneath a thick layer of slippery powder. Just before finishing her dinner Rosalie had called Alphonse and asked him for his help. Alphonse had found his usual automobile less than fit for the journey, and yet here he was before them, all smiles, in a car he had dutifully rented from a local mechanic.[10]

Six inches of wet snow blanketed the roads Alphonse, squinting into the snowbound darkness, endeavored to follow.[11] Twice within the first couple of miles the pilgrims' trusty chauffeur nearly skidded off the road. Each time Rosalie felt her heart leap in her chest, and each time their driver somehow managed to steer the vehicle back onto the icy highway. Ahead, the car's headlights illuminated the dangerous bend in the road back to Valatie, and Rosalie found herself bracing for the curve even before Alphonse cranked the wheel.

The General screamed as she felt the car leave the road.

When she opened her eyes, she saw Ida and Lavinia, wild-eyed with fear, beside her. Had it not been for a single miraculously placed tree stump, the General realized, peering down into the dark chasm below them, her little band would surely have met their deaths. Rosalie was startled to see Alphonse's once-proud rental badly damaged and hanging at a forty-five degree angle over the embankment.

Collectively, they held their breath as the car hung suspended. To move was to risk tipping the already precariously perched automobile downward into a deadly tumble, but what else could they do? Slowly, they scooted to the car's upper side, hoping to tip its balance in their favor for the brief moments required to climb out of the car to safety. Inch by inch they shifted their weight until at last the pilgrims had planted their feet again on terra firma.

The suffragettes, thank heavens, were safe. The time read 7:30.[12]

Suffragist headquarters in Manhattan had wanted a bold, headline-generating incident from Rosalie Jones's army, but never had any of them imagined that the big black type of tomorrow would read, "Women Have Narrow Escape from Injury When Auto Skids on 20-foot Embankment."[13]

Once again fate had smiled on the faithful pilgrims. All the avowed Antis who had not-so-secretly wished the suffragettes would simply go away had nearly gotten their wish, Rosalie noted ruefully. She peered down the road in the direction from which they had come, hoping against hope that another driver would be out on a dreadful night in which the wet snow had changed over into a rainstorm.[14]

Exactly how many drenching, chilly moments passed she could not be certain, but in time Rosalie saw a pair of headlights careening down the curvy road toward them. When the car stopped, Rosalie asked if the driver would be so kind as to take them back to the inn. She introduced her officers and their cause with the earnest hope that this Good Samaritan and his passenger would lend a helping hand regardless of their views on votes for women.

Mercifully, the Good Samaritan dropped Rosalie and her officers at the hotel, asking nothing for his troubles. Before she could so much as inquire after his name or the name of his passenger, the reporters who'd stayed behind at the inn fairly swarmed the General with questions:

Where on earth had she been, and why was she so thoroughly soaked?!

"I don't know if that poor driver is lying frozen in the middle of the road," Rosalie lamented.[15] The reporters seemed only to care about General Jones and her fellow officers, but all Rosalie could think of was her brush with death and the kind man who had gone out of his way, quite literally, to help the pilgrims.

And still the war correspondents, eager for headlines, wanted only to know: Would the car wreck suspend the march? Were the General and her officers well enough to continue the hike until its conclusion?

Rosalie confessed that her arm was bruised but that she was otherwise in good condition. Perhaps the accident had been a wake-up call, she added, and a "tonic" to help remind them of the bigger picture.[16] The weather conditions between now and the end of the march seemed destined to get even more challenging, and rather than risk becoming snowbound in the rugged terrain around Valatie, the accident had alerted the suffrage pilgrims to the need to make haste for the capital.

"We are going through," the General insisted.[17] "It is eighteen miles, but we are tired of… doing only four or five miles a day…. Our first plan was to reach the capital on New Year's Eve," she told them, and here was a headline they would do well to print in bold type: The General and her officers had formally decided that they would hasten rather than delay their schedule, a few scratches and bruises be damned! "[Surgeon] General Dock insisted that her feet, which were our only concern, would be equal to the tramp."

Rosalie's army would live to fight another day, and a fateful day it would be!

"We will do as the army of the people did at Jericho," added General Jones. "We will march around the state capitol several times, just as the ancients marched around the temple in Jericho several times, and we will raise a mighty shout, although ours will be a shout of 'Votes for women.'"[18]

The news sent the journalists scurrying to their quarters to peck out their copy for the next morning. Headline: *General Claims Surgeon General Well Enough to Tramp on to Albany!* Headline: *Suffragette General Suffers Car Wreck; Shaken and Stirred*; Headline: *Suffragists to Cele-*

brate New Year Two Days Early! But despite these hysterics, the reporters overlooked the full ramifications of Rosalie's startling announcement, for everyone who had planned to travel to the capital to share in the pilgrims' moment of glory needed to be put on notice; they had better catch an early train if they wanted to bathe in the limelight.[19] And this included that chain-smoking, hard-drinking, militant British suffragette Inez Craven who had been threatening to rejoin since Peekskill and now threatened to steal the show from the pilgrims who had actually walked the walk.

The marchers' decision also served notice to the more respected suffrage dignitaries such as Nora Blatch De Forest, who had been one of the original signatories to the message still safely tucked away in Rosalie's knapsack for delivery to the Governor. Mrs. De Forest was the granddaughter of Elizabeth Cady Stanton, the leader of the early women's rights movement and the author of the Declaration of Sentiments at the famous Seneca Falls Convention. In many ways Mrs. Stanton was the queen mother of the American suffragist movement, which made her granddaughter Nora something of a princess one step removed. Nora's mother, Harriet Stanton Blatch, had kindly mentored Rosalie prior to her first large-scale suffrage speech at the corner of Wall Street, the one in which the mostly male audience had tossed eggs and tomatoes at her. Rosalie could only hope that her army's decision to push ahead to arrive in Albany two days ahead of schedule would not upset Harriet or Nora, or make Nora feel as if she had been upstaged without warning.

They had walked nearly 155 miles from 242nd street in the Bronx, including detours, in nearly two weeks' time. They were now, the General noted, within eighteen miles of the capital — and of the Governor-elect whose attention they hoped to capture.

CHAPTER 10:
ALBANY OR BUST!

What's the matter with Dock, brave, dear Dock?
What's the matter with Dock, Dock, Dock, Dock?

Normally it was Jessie who generated the marching songs for Rosalie's army, but today — the last day of the march to the capital, if all went well — the General took it upon herself to improvise the motivational ditty for her eldest foot soldier.[1]

Indeed, what was the matter with Lavinia Dock? The usually indomitable Surgeon General had lagged behind since they'd left Valatie earlier that morning, so much so that Rosalie had called periodic halts to the march to allow the good nurse to catch up. The hike had battered and bruised them all, even the youthful Gladys and Rosalie. Boots had been patched and re-patched so many times they now threatened to disappear in tatters. Heavy rains overnight had turned the road leading out of Valatie into clay so wet it splashed over the tops of the suffragettes' boots and soaked into their socks.[2]

Still and all, the march continued. Rosalie's troops now found themselves hiking through the shortest days of the year, and not even an 8:45 departure time that chilly morning could guarantee them an arrival in the capital by nightfall, especially not with frequent stops.[3] When the silly ditty they'd concocted to put a spring back in the step of Lavinia Dock grew old, Rosalie led her troops in a rendition of Wagner's famous folk song "Pilgrims' Chorus":[4]

> Blessed, I may now look on thee, oh, my native land,
> and gladly greet thy pleasant pastures;
> now I lay my pilgrim's staff aside to rest,
> because, faithful to God, I have completed my pilgrimage![5]

Rosalie hoped the spiritual strains of "Pilgrims' Chorus" would bring her group back together in lockstep. That very morning she — or perhaps it was more accurate to say the press corps following the army — had detected some discord in the ranks, and it had begun with dear Dock. The General did not rightly care what the press corps thought of her decision to push on and arrive early. Their desire to draw out the march another day or two to increase newsstand sales back home in the cities from whence they came did not interest her as much as reaching their destination. Ida concurred, when they had discussed it as a group, and the battle lines had thus been drawn. Lavinia and Jessie had balked, however, suggesting as politely as they could to Rosalie that she ought to be more concerned with the press, who were ultimately the vehicle by which to reach the people.

"The pilgrims reached here with nerves stretched to the breaking point," the *New York Times* reporter wrote. "There was evidence of strained relations when the army took up the march this morning."[6] Rosalie might not have chosen exactly those words, but it was true — a confident, self-assured leader must endure occasional challenges to her leadership, especially if she is young. The newspaper further commented, "Until yesterday it had been hard to know just who was in command of the army," and perhaps that was true as well. Rosalie believed in being a general more than a dictator; if being a leader necessitated being a dictator, she wanted no part of it. To a woman, her troops were smart, accomplished, savvy, determined, and steadfast; in short, they were not the sort, in Rosalie's eyes, who benefited from much bossing.

And that's where the improvised marching song had come in: "What's the matter with Dock, brave, dear Dock?" It had been Rosalie's peace offering to the unflagging Surgeon General, and also a rallying cry for unity as they crested Clinton Heights. For the first time, in nearly 175 miles marched, they saw with their own eyes the precious sight of the capital laid out before them. A cheer went up from the army. It was 3:30 p.m.

In her khaki skirts and long overcoat drawn tightly against the cold, Rosalie stopped to address her troops. "Comrades," she said, "behold our goal! For thirteen days we have tramped through rain and snow to bring from the great city of New York to the chief executive of this state a message of woman's emancipation. We have endured hardship, privation, and pain that the cause of woman's suffrage be given new impetus."[7]

It was hard not to be excited, relieved, and maybe a bit crestfallen, too, to find their most immediate journey near its end. After days in the woods, the image of the great sprawling city awaiting them jarred their collective senses. The capital meant lawyers, lawmakers, and lobbyists; it meant couriers and chauffeurs and meetings behind closed doors. It meant the "man-made" world with all its intrigue and treachery.

But the city also meant clean linens and laundry soap smelling of lavender. It meant new mail from friends and family and hugs from enthusiastic supporters. It meant that home — New York City — would only be a train-ride away. But most of all it meant that they had arrived at their destination — the appointed time and the appointed place to which history had called them forth as activists and witnesses. Practically, it meant that they would be able to deliver their message to the Governor-elect if they could just track him down, and they would; Rosalie was determined.

All that lay before them in a city that in two hours would be covered in darkness. Before the pilgrims stretched the Rensselaer toll bridge, making it seem as if their entry into the city of destiny was itself a fairy tale written by some greater hand. At the bridge over the Hudson River rushing with new snowmelt, Dr. Culver of the Men's League for Equal Suffrage of Albany stood waiting to meet them. He was positively beamish, insisting that his organization pay the pilgrims' toll into the city. Dr. Culver had been a supporter of the votes-for-women cause for nearly fifty years, and he could hardly contain his excitement. Rosalie smiled at his gesture of support, for in addition to its goodness, it allowed her to stay true to her pledge that no fee should be paid for transportation anywhere along their route; after all, theirs was a march into the history books, not a complimentary lift. Accompanying the good doctor were two police officers dispatched to escort Rosalie's band safely into the capital city.

General Jones led the way with her head held high.[8] Gladys walked with the natural gait of an athlete. Ida looked the part of the suffragette in her yellow hat and yellow boots. Lavinia walked with a new spring in her step, despite her arthritis and tired ankles.[9] And Jessie carried her staff that bore the inscription "The Truth Against the World."[10]

After crossing the bridge, the pilgrims marched single-file into the streets of Albany. The clock read 4:00 p.m.[11] Crowds gathered for two full city blocks to greet them. As the marching suffragettes turned down State Street, the General ordered her weary travelers to a sudden halt. "There is the Capitol," she said, waving her staff in its direction. And behind her the army cheered.[12]

The building itself looked like a dream, like an image they had only dared to imagine previously, the very same that, during their darkest moments on the trail, had brought them back from the edge of hopelessness.

As they marched down State Street the sheer size of the crowds made it difficult for the troops to keep their line. Word had gone out that Rosalie's army had arrived to "capture" the Governor, and everyone, it seemed, wanted to witness history on the march. Traffic came to a standstill. Whistles screeched, bells chimed, car horns blared in celebration.[13] Saturday shoppers crowded the street, but the gravity of the pilgrims' cause parted the hustle and bustle, creating a long lane of applauding men, women, and children. Even the "street urchins" found voice enough to cry out: "I'll vote for you when I grow up!"[14] Elsewhere along the broad avenue, homes signaled their welcome. Families draped their smallest children in the American flag; children rang bells to herald the pilgrims' coming; mothers handed Rosalie's suffragettes baskets full of fresh apples.

General Jones finally brought her troops to a halt in front of the Hampton Hotel that would be their headquarters. She readied herself as the photographers crouched to take her picture, and the newspaper reporters jostled to record her every word. The time was 4:40, and a dramatic dusk had descended upon the Capitol.

"Our task has been accomplished," Rosalie declared, trying her best to sound like a determined general again instead of a very weary, very footsore girl.[15] "We have done the thing that we set out to do, and in that thought alone there is much satisfaction. But we have had to do more than that. We have had a chance to talk to the men and women of the rural districts. They have come to know us, and many of them believe in us and in the cause we represent. In this we have accomplished much, but how much more good have we done when one thinks of the women who now understand us as missionaries to the cause."

Rosalie stopped to gather herself, her breath now visible in the brisk air. "I should like to have everybody form a New Year's resolution that they shall at least consider seriously the proposition of votes for women…. We feel that we have touched the people along the line of march in a way that could have been effective by no other method. We feel that the people realize that this is no idle notion. A pilgrimage has always stood for the highest ideals of the cause it represents, and we are sure from the receptions we have been accorded that our march has not been in vain."[16]

A pilgrimage it was, and a pilgrimage it would remain. That was just the word, for this was a quest to seek the constitutionally implied right of a woman's vote — a right the vast majority of Rosalie's countrywomen had never experienced but that somehow had become a reality in some future world, where women worked and voted alongside men without doubt or awkwardness, fear, or envy. And like most pilgrims it was the faith they held in their hearts — the powerful faith in the not yet seen but keenly felt— that had moved them forward on feet that not so long ago had refused to believe.

CHAPTER 11:
IN THE FIGHT!

———————

Timing. Everything was timing, Rosalie realized.

For nearly two weeks Rosalie's army had found itself racing against time to reach the capital, and now, just as suddenly, they had a surplus of hours. So diligent had the General been in her efforts to keep her march on and ahead of schedule, she had orchestrated an arrival on December 28, two days early!

Now, a day after their triumph, time turned temporarily back into an obstacle. The war correspondents who had traveled with Rosalie's band were eager to return to their families, and the reporters newly arrived to cover the suffragettes' arrival in Albany were growing restless for want of news.

Time, however, afforded Rosalie the chance to sleep the sleep of the just; and for Gladys Coursen, it provided the opportunity to perform a reconnaissance walk around the Capitol building.[1] For Jessie Hardy Stubbs, these unapportioned hours offered the chance to write her long-overdue letter to her editors at *Woman's Journal*, who stood waiting, like the rest of the nation, for updates from the front.

"We have been showered with blessings, congratulations, and God-speeds," Jessie wrote, burning the last of the energy she held in reserve.[2] "If we are somewhat tired, it is due not to the length of the journey, but to the unusual strain upon the pilgrims in other directions. We all of us realized, and have repeated over and over again, that we were not walking any more or even as much as the longest "hike" that thousands of American working women walk every day on their jobs. The only difference between the pilgrims and the working women is that the pilgrims had God's outdoors and nothing to carry but an Alpen staff, while the great army of women in the industrial world are carrying all kinds of burdens and standing on their feet twelve and fourteen hours a day, and there is no popular acclaim for them."

Time allowed the pilgrims to reach out to the congregants of the many churches of Albany, hoping to explain their journey, pilgrim-to-pilgrim, and win over still more converts. Already, however, the bishop of Albany, Reverend William Croswell Doane, had publicly criticized Rosalie's army, saying, "I have no faith in the cause of the suffragists. The women themselves are not as ill-behaved as their sisters in England, but they are directed by the same impulse. This demonstration will not help their cause any."[3]

General Jones had been quick to react to the bishop's criticism, pointing out that that the bishop's own daughter, Margaret, was a well-known Anti. "If we are making a display of ourselves she is doing the same thing by making speeches against the cause," Rosalie said in spirited defense of her troops. The refusals by many churches to listen to the votes-for-women appeals hurt and confused Rosalie, herself the product of a religious family. If the good people of the cloth could not be counted on to support the health and welfare of their women congregants, who could be counted on? If not God, then government? And if neither, then whom? She was especially aggrieved by the fact that Ida had been turned down by the Calvary Baptist Church on the grounds that the clergy there had not wanted to "open any such question in the church."

But, dear Clergymen, don't you see the question has already been opened! Rosalie badly wished to proclaim. *Opened by a thousand brave women requesting that the promise of the Constitution be extended them as citizens.* Everything, it seemed, required more time than a woman like Rosalie Gardiner Jones was wont to provide.

But time also meant precious moments here and there squirreled away for a niceties seldom available to the troops on the trail: like reading the newspaper cover to cover. It never ceased to amaze the troops how much of the day's crop of sensational news involved some barely acknowledged violence against, or abject disregard for, women. Yesterday's newpapers alone included such troubling headlines as "Girl Shipped As Freight"; "Kills Mother-in-Law Then Lays Down to Sleep"; "Charged with Murder of Six, Wife Says Not Guilty"; and "Jealous Boy Kills Girl: Lad of Fifteen Shoots Clara LeMay, Aged Fourteen, And Then Commits Suicide."[4] The headline reading "Deaf Mute Stabs

Woman to Death When She Scorns Him" was even more chilling.[5] And not so very far from here in Buffalo, New York, "pretty Julia Goodie" (and why was it that newspapers always insisted on remarking on a woman's appearance?) had refused the wooing of one John Valiquete, and her would-be suitor had responded by plunging a dagger three times into the young woman's chest.

And still somehow America's newspapers pushed men and women relentlessly toward marriage. The day's harvest of headlines had also included the curious caption "Former 'Stork' Mayor to Introduce Bachelor Bill." State Senator Edmund Beall's bachelor bill had proposed requiring unmarried men of a certain age to pay $100 a year in taxes for failing to marry a young woman and instead "running at large." "These young buck ought to be married…. What good are they?" the senator had asked. "Let them pay a tax and let it go for the support of some of their progressive brothers who are raising families." And yet the senator had failed even to consider the notion that not all men were meant to be fathers, just as not all women were suited to marriage and motherhood, or desirous of it.

Not all the news of the day was troubling for young women, however. The New York City garment workers (whose cause many of the suffragettes had taken up alongside their own) had voted to go on strike against intolerable conditions and low wages. In nearby Boston an organizer for the Ladies' Garment Workers' Union had just yesterday asked for a grand jury to investigate the working conditions for girls. The district attorney would be asked to present evidence showing that hundreds of girls in that city had been working sixty to eighty hours a week in tenement sweatshops under what the newspaper described as "frightful conditions." And of course it wasn't just young girls and women who were suffering, but men as well. The very same papers that had carried news of pro-women's welfare strikes and grand juries had reported that seventeen thousand men in Chicago were living on a mere twenty cents a day. Headlines like these reminded even the most ardent suffragists that their cause was the cause of the disenfranchised, wherever they lived and whatever their sex.

The very same newspaper that had trumpeted the arrival of Rosalie's army had also celebrated the good news that Mr. Andrew Carnegie,

America's greatest philanthropist, had pledged an additional $25 million to charities, raising his total donation to $205 million. Mr. John D. Rockefeller of New York followed a close second, with $185 million to "various helpful enterprises."[6] Rosalie may have wished that among these endeavors deemed worthy would be the cause of votes for women. And yet a true leader learned not to hold her breath, or to wait on other people's money in order to act her conscience.

Rosalie's and Ida's and Katherine's and Lavinia's hometown of New York City could always be counted on for splashy bold type, and today was no exception. After weeks of speculation that William Rockefeller had escaped to the woods of upstate New York — the very woods through which the pilgrims had tramped — he had been found hiding out in his 5th Avenue residence.[7] The Sergeant-at-Arms of the House of Representatives who had hunted the business mogul like a hound these last few weeks had threatened to serve Mr. Rockefeller with a subpoena requiring him to testify before Congress concerning dodgy deals in his copper mines out West. Mr. Rockefeller had avoided being served papers for weeks by disguising himself, almost comically, in oversized ear mufflers and goggles, slinking low in the driver's seat whenever he motored away from the premises in order to evade detection.

Then came the story of the capture and identification of the elusive arsonist back in Brooklyn. The arsonist turned out to be one Grace Trimble, sixteen years old, who had attempted to set fire to the building at 214 Kingston Avenue no less than seven times. When questioned by the police upon her arrest, Miss Trimble had said, "I don't know why I did it, only I just love to watch the flames. The blaze is so pretty."[8]

While she could never condone the lawlessness of Miss Trimble's actions, a pilgrim of Rosalie's army could be imagined to understand such a sentiment while she waited hours and days for an audience with the Governor-elect. Sometimes, setting fire to a status quo possessed a strange beauty all its own.

There was time, too, for the pilgrims to laugh at themselves, and even sometimes at their own misfortune. One recent advertisement in the *New York Times* proclaimed "Suffrage Hikers Were Near Death When the Chainless Tires of Their Auto Skidded."[9] Labeled as a "Special Notice," it read exactly like many of the other *Times* news stories about their march, until Rosalie reached the third paragraph from the end, which noted: "If the tires of the car had been equipped with WEED ANTI-SKID CHAINS the accident would not have occurred…. Stop off at your dealer today and fully equip your car with WEED CHAINS."

The ad had been taken out by Weed Chain Tire Grip Company of New York. Where else but in America would the army's near-tragedy become, a mere two days later, a way to turn a quick profit!

The unexpected surplus of time also meant that the pilgrims now had a hard time avoiding the incessant questions of an increasingly anxious press. In the made-for-headlines, pie-in-the-sky scenarios the press envisioned, the state's chief executive would have met the General immediately upon her crossing the bridge to Albany, and, with much ado and great flourish, signed suffrage into law right there on the spot.

Rosalie knew, however, that neither the new Governor, nor her army, nor anyone else, for that matter, had the power to wave a magic wand and instantly grant the women of New York the right to vote. First, legislation would need to be introduced to the state legislature, at the Governor's initiative, where it would be endlessly debated and, if passed, ultimately put to a vote of the people of New York. Political and social change was a process, not merely a destination. It was a journey.

General Jones reminded the members of the press that a "spectacular march" had been a necessity to draw the attention of a state, and a nation, to their cause.[10] As far away as the West Coast, newspaper editors had concluded that the hike had "awakened the Empire State," with the *San Francisco Call* warning, "If Governor-elect William Sulzer does not smile on the movement his official life will be made miserable and his path strewn with thorns."[11] Rosalie would, she said, be remiss not to thank the journalists for their part in making it so impactful — especially the "war correspondents" who had traveled with the pilgrims in order to better tell their tale.[12]

The press, however, was not content with the laurels the General laid at their feet; it wanted what the press always wanted: answers. More specifically, they wanted the scoop on when, exactly, Rosalie intended to deliver the secret message she had carried with her to give in-person to the Governor-elect.

The plan was this, she told them: A platoon of Rosalie's army consisting of Alice, Lavinia, Katherine, and tramper-reporter Sibyl Wibur would be dispatched to the train station to shadow the would-be Governor at a respectful distance upon his arrival in town.[13] Sibyl and Katherine would use their trained reporters' eyes to scan passing faces in the crowded train station, on high alert for anyone in the future Governor's advance party. Once advised of his whereabouts, the General would dispatch the youngest member of her army, Gladys, to the executive's door to request an interview between the General and the Governor. Since joining in Poughkeepsie, Gladys had been promoted to "Chief Aid" to the General.[14] The soon-to-be Governor would be under constant surveillance by army scouts until he formally accepted an in-person interview with Rosalie.

General Jones and her marching suffragettes weren't about to take no for an answer.

Still, beyond the overall unity of their purpose, Rosalie had sensed her pilgrims' unique single-mindedness beginning to fray. The *New York Press* had run an oversized montage of the suffragettes as they marched into Albany — pictures that had shown Rosalie bundled up against the cold but otherwise all smiles; Colonel Craft striding bravely forward with the Alpine staff Rosalie had given her in hand, a contented pilgrim in the snow; Gladys Coursen sledding happily atop a toboggan. And yet the words of the *Press* told a less superficial story, and one perhaps nearer the truth. "It was with a sigh of relief that General Jones spoke of disbanding the 'army' tomorrow," the article read. "No other comment was needed as to her private opinion of the squabbling that has cast gloom over all since the arrival."

Surely some of the bickering had carried over since the disagreement at Valatie over Rosalie's decision to march into the capital city early, but it had worsened when Rosalie announced that after delivering their message she might indeed like to return to the life of a "civilian" at least for a few days. "After we disband," she cautioned them, "I will not be General Jones, but Miss Jones."

Some of her officers, like Lavinia, thought it proper to wear dour faces until the Governor had conceded to their requests. What message would Rosalie be sending if she danced at the inaugural ball while (and if) the Governor had agreed to do nothing more than meet with them? And, adding insult to injury, today Bishop Doane had called the suffragettes "silly women" — fighting words that so angered Ida that for a time she could not concentrate on anything else. Meanwhile, some of the New York City suffragists had moved in to either steal the spotlight from, or else patronizingly judge, Rosalie and her army. Mary Garrett Hay had been quoted as saying, "It isn't necessary to chase to Albany or hound the Governor-elect…. I am willing to take his word. No use in chasing after him."[15] Meanwhile, Nora Blatch De Forest, no doubt a bit envious of the attention Rosalie's marching suffragettes had been paid, had called their hike "a picturesque thing to do" and referred to it as "splendid to stir up sentiment," but had then initiated her own attempt to meet with the Governor-to-be first — before Rosalie and her army could get to him!

Splendid?! Picturesque?! After sacrificing her health and well-being to walk 175 miles all told, Rosalie couldn't be blamed if she was a bit indignant at the high-handed treatment from some. But the General knew there was no need to get angry, for she knew two important things: first, that Gladys would be able to succeed in wrangling the Governor-elect into an in-person meeting; and second, that there would be more marching days to come.

And then there was this simple fact: Rosalie did not herself *need* the spotlight, even if her cause did. It was not good for the psyche to have a title precede you your entire life. The army's march together had been grand indeed, but she neither needed nor wanted illusions of grandeur. She had led a first-of-its-kind, history-making march to improve her country, yes, but she was also a young woman perfectly comfortable stepping out of the limelight for a time. The star of the march must not be a person, but the sacred cause that had kept their feet moving and their hearts full all along.

✿ ✿ ✿

Time moved slowly and quickly all at once as the suffragettes waited to ambush the new Governor with their message. Like a good waltz rhythm it moved slow then quick, quick, then slow again. Today, December 29, had thus far been as fleeting as a candle flame and simultaneously as long as a lifetime, and it had brought with it the most personal of revelations.

Inspired by the poignancy of the moment before them, Jessie Hardy Stubbs grabbed her pen and sat down to do what she did best: write. A poem rather than a news story, she decided, was required to record for posterity the fighting spirit of her fellow soldiers. After much thought she decided to title her verse "In the Fight!" When she was through, she sat back in her chair and read its final lines aloud to be sure it was right:

> Hail, comrades, in the fight!
> Keep looking toward the light,
>   Justice we call!
> Strong let our courage be;
> Man is about to see
> Our country must be free[16]

If Jessie was feeling a little emotional as she composed the climactic lines of her commemorative verse, who could blame her? In her possession she also had another very important dispatch — one so unlikely that she had had to read it over and over again to believe that it was real. Earlier in the day she had received at the Hampton Hotel an unsolicited letter. Her very own name — *Hardy* — had been printed at the top of the return address in a bold masculine hand. Even before she'd opened the missive she'd felt her usually sturdy knees growing weak, and, when she saw the note's contents, they'd buckled altogether.

Her father!

How old had she been when last she heard his voice or felt his embrace? She could have been no more than eight, she reasoned.[17] The war correspondents around her at the time had reported that she had collapsed from "sheer joy," and perhaps it was true, but now, hours later, she suspected the jubilation she'd felt upon breaking the seal of the letter was no simple kind of joy. For had there not been some shocked indignation and a bit of long-simmering anger in it, too? She had not heard from her father in twenty-five years, and now, at a moment of personal triumph, he suddenly wanted back into her life.[18] Granted, it had been her mother's decision, as well as his, for the two to separate and for her mother to move east, but her father — well, even the newspapers were saying Major A. L. Hardy had "dropped out of sight as if swallowed up by the earth."[19] He had, in the intervening years, developed a reputation as a prominent newspaper editor in Illinois — the very profession Jessie had chosen as her own. How much might she have learned from him years ago in embarking on her own career as a journalist? How badly had she wanted him at her wedding, and yet for all this idle wishing she had received nothing but silence from him.

And now here, stuffed in an envelope, were clippings of a life whose details had been all but unknown to her. He had written several books, the clippings revealed, including two histories of his adopted hometown of Pittsburgh, where he was living now and where he had been a historian of the Carnegie Library. A retired major in the Army, he had graduated from the very military academy in Peekskill that Jessie and the pilgrims had passed on their march, ignorant of its significance, a mere handful of days ago on the most arduous leg of their journey — the one in which they had felt most like giving up.

She read the letter again, unable to come to terms just yet with the unexpected warmth of its sentiments: "I am proud of the position you have acquired," her father had written. "Hope to hear from you soon." Still earlier in the afternoon, upon recovering from the shock and regaining her voice, she'd vowed to the war correspondents that she would get back in communication with him as soon as the suffrage message was safely delivered into the hands of the Governor-elect. Bygones must be allowed to be bygones if human beings, that most grudge-holding of all species, would ever truly progress. And what better time than today, the day before New Year's Eve day, to embrace the future in lieu of the past?

"No matter what fruit the pilgrimage may bear," Jessie told the reporters, "it has done one thing that fills my heart with joy today — it has restored my father to me, and that is the greatest gift that heaven could bestow upon me."

Indeed, had Jessie stayed home from the march, as she had been tempted to do, making her occasional lectures on behalf of votes for women, she very much doubted that her father would have decided to reach out to her, for he had learned of her whereabouts via newspaper coverage of the hike. But now, on the cusp of delivering their fateful message to the most powerful man in the state, her long-lost father had been moved to put pen to paper. In joining the march Jessie had acted bravely and independently, and in his own small way, her father was attempting to follow her example, step by brave step.

Fame was unaccountable and strange, Jessie realized, but it was also generous, making possible all manner of blessed serendipity.[20] How many times along their snowy route had Jessie and her fellow pilgrims wondered whether they would indeed have a roof over their heads that night? And yet each time, as if in answer to their prayers, it seemed some Good Samaritan emerged from nowhere, offering the travelers space in their home.

The march had been fated to occur, Jessie and the other pilgrims believed, destined to create lasting connections born of seemingly random encounters. Despite anything that might have been alleged by the Antis, the suffrage hike had been about building bridges, not burning them.

☼   ☼   ☼

Christmas had come and gone for the suffrage pilgrims and yet today, December 30, had felt very much like the advent of that blessed season. They were breathless with anticipation and nervous with anxiety all at once. It had been a busy day for Rosalie and her army, culminating in a presentation to the Albany Suffragette Club titled "Pilgrim's Tales" in a mass meeting at the Historical and Art Society Building. Everyone, it seemed, wanted to hear their story — what they had seen on their long and difficult journey, what joys and sorrows they had held in their hearts along the road, how they had kept the small flame inside them burning despite the wintry chill and the endless miles. Naturally, Rosalie had taken the podium first, but what on earth could she say about an event — a happening really — that absolutely defied description? She decided she would title her talk "Old Maid's Tale" and speak to just how far women had come from the days when they were valued mostly for cooking and cleaning, and how far, paradoxically, they still had yet to travel on their journey toward equality.

Still, an old maid's tale didn't quite seem to capture it, for, after all, Rosalie was still young. And despite a fatigue so extreme she could not properly name it, she had never felt quite so full of life. No, the kind of gratitude she was feeling required her loyal friend and steadfast sister suffragette, Ida, to properly put into words.

When at last they found a quite space to sit together and consider, Rosalie and Ida attempted to find language for the feelings of fullness within incompleteness they were both experiencing. Their mission still hung in the balance, it was true, and yet their feelings of gratitude were undeniable. Gratitude did not depend on success, any more than pilgrims depended on guarantees when they set off on uncertain journeys in good faith.

Gratitude meant, for example, that even though Rosalie had received a telegram from her mother earlier in the day that had *still* failed to support her and her cause,[21] the General nevertheless felt grateful to have arrived safely at the end of a long journey that was, paradoxically, just the beginning of history's larger march toward women's equality. Gratitude meant appreciating that Ida's hometown newspaper back in Brooklyn, the *Daily Eagle*, had invited the two friends to issue suffrage supporters back home a heartfelt New Year's message, and they gratefully accepted. Together they wrote:

> We take this opportunity, through the courtesy of the
> *Daily Eagle*, to assure our Brooklyn friends that New
> Year greetings is not a hollow, meaningless phrase. The
> prospects for suffrage are better than ever before. This trip
> through the country has given us an insight into the state

of suffrage sentiment… which has been a constant delight. Everywhere we found interest just waiting to be crystallized into real suffrage enthusiasm. The people came to their doors and open windows to wish us Godspeed.

There was little ridicule and no open hostility. Of course we cannot say that everybody we saw was a believer in women's cause, but the attitude even of the anti-suffragists is best explained by incidents such as this.

It was the day we walked from Peekskill to Fishkill, twenty-two miles, through six-inch mud, with a cold rain beating in our faces. In the muddiest corner of the country road we met two men, evidently residents of the nearby farms. They gave us cheery greetings and as they passed we heard one say, "Gee whiz, Bill, they're doin' more for their cause than we men would."

On this trip hundreds of people have heard the votes-for-women gospel whom we never could have reached through ordinary meetings. We distributed thousands of rainbow leaflets at farm house doors, and made immediate speeches at crossroads gatherings…

Awake, sisters, and help us. It won't do to sit back and say, "Yes, I think women ought to vote." We must pack up our knapsacks and say, "We've got to get it."

Wishing you all could have had the inspiration of this pilgrimage, we are yours for the cause.[22]

—*Rosalie Gardiner Jones and Ida C. Craft*

New Year's Eve day, 1:50 p.m.: At long last the Governor-elect of perhaps the most powerful state in America had arrived at the train station! And the secret scouts in Rosalie's indefatigable army had tracked his every move like so many gumshoes.

As soon as word reached the officers' makeshift headquarters at the Hampton Hotel, Rosalie gave the order to march upon the Governor's mansion to intercept the state's chief executive before he slipped through their grasp. The General stuck carefully to her plan, sending

Gladys to knock on the door to the Governor's residence while she and the other marchers waited on the lawn at a discreet distance.

Rosalie's heart sank, though, when she saw the heavy door open not to William L. Sulzer but to his chief military aid, Major Schermerhorn.[23]

General Jones looked on, crestfallen, as the Major disappeared, closing the heavy door behind him. It seemed impossible — no one had ever turned down Gladys before! Behind her Rosalie could feel the morale of her tireless troopers drop precipitously. But before she could summon the words to console them the big door of the manse swung open a second time to reveal not just the Major but also the Governor himself! And he was walking briskly toward where Rosalie stood firmly on the executive lawn. He wore a black coat with a waistcoat, and underneath that a high-collared shirt with an unadorned black tie. William L. Sulzer was known for his unassuming gray coats, and here, too, Rosalie, who had preferred to wear common khaki during her march, felt some commonality. The General did not believe in foppery or high dress; if a woman was earnest about her business and her cause, she would let the cause, not her fashion, get top billing.

True to form, on this day "Plain Bill" Sulzer had dressed simply for the impromptu meeting. Incredibly, he had made Rosalie's army the first order of business upon arriving at the Governor's mansion![24]

Still, if the news reports were true, the People's Governor was in a mood to reject, rather than to approve. Some said he had arrived with a chip on his shoulder and a desire to control the wasteful excesses of government and reign in the corrupt Tammany Hall organization that had, nevertheless, been instrumental in his election.

Sometimes a leader must split from even their friends and allies, Rosalie knew, when still more dramatic action needed taking. Already, Sulzer had rejected the request by certain New York City officials to raise their own pay, and had given the all-powerful Tammany political machine boss Charles Murphy a stern talking to.[25] Now, judging by the look on his face, he appeared ready to reject any new requests from the all-woman army that had besieged him.

After the two would-be executives — one a governor-to-be, the other a general of a platoon of suffragettes — exchanged greetings,

Rosalie remembered the message she had clutched in her hand on the march up the hill to the Governor's mansion. It was the carefully sealed note that the most important suffragists in the most influential state in the Union had entrusted her to carry nearly 175 miles on foot, through snow and ice and wind, across lonesome woods punctuated by the sound of gunshots and menaced by escaped convicts and industrial barons on the lam. Here it was, after so many miles, the suffrage parchment framed in mission wood, written in her hand and trembling in her fingers.[26] Keeping the Governor-to-be steadily in her gaze, she surrendered the scroll to him, and watched with anticipation, hopefulness, and no small amount of dread as the next leader of the most powerful state in America read a missive whose simple boldness captured the spirit of the movement:

> The suffrage hosts of the Empire State send greetings and renewed congratulations to Governor William L. Sulzer and express the earnest hope that his administration may be distinguished by the speedy passage of the woman's suffrage amendment.[27]

The simple note was signed in part "The Cooperative Committee," for there had been many authors of its sentiments, not just one. Sulzer turned the framed message over in his hands, and read the additional message he found inscribed there: "Votes for women pilgrims carried this message on foot from New York to Albany, having left Monday, December 16, in order to greet the Governor-elect upon his arrival at the Capitol."[28]

Sulzer's eyebrows furrowed for a moment, and General Jones could feel her army, standing behind her, grow tense. After what seemed a never-ending pause, the man scheduled to be sworn in as Governor the very next day shook his head and said solemnly, "I think you have made a mistake."[29]

A mistake? The words sent the General's mind whirling. The message had been gone over many times back at headquarters in Manhattan. What could possibly be mistaken? Before her now, the Governor-elect continued, "This is for William L. Sulzer." He stopped to emphasize the middle initial, adding, matter-of-factly, "This is not my name."

For a long moment Rosalie wondered what exactly she ought to say. She was certain the committee had recorded his name correctly! Dare she correct the state's highest public official on the matter of his own name, after insolently marching onto the grounds of his mansion and demanding an audience with him?

"That's not my name," the imposing man repeated. Again, the executive surveyed the youthful General Jones with those uncannily discerning eyes — eyes that seemed to cut right through her. "My name is Plain Bill Sulzer."

Of course! Rosalie realized her "mistake" at once, inwardly rejoicing. William L. Sulzer was to be the People's Governor, and had been known as "Plain Bill" since his earliest days as a politician fighting for the plain and often voiceless people of his great state.

"All my life," Plain Bill added, "I have believed in the right of women to have the [vote] as a matter of political justice. In the future as in the past I will do all I can to advance the political rights of women. I have incorporated in my message to the legislature the advice that the suffrage amendment be adopted. I also hope it will be adopted by the people."

How sweet those words sounded to Rosalie's ears, and how much sweeter to have come from the lips of the man most capable of giving those sentiments life, provided he had the support of the people in helping bring them to fruition.

The General felt a great weight temporarily lifted from her shoulders as Plain Bill honored her army's unlikely efforts, efforts that had not been a sacrifice at all, but a calling. "You… deserve commendation for your enthusiasm for a great cause that ought to be respected by everybody…. I congratulate you on the successful outcome of your pilgrimage and assure you that in the future, as in the past, all I can do for your cause will be done." And with that, the Governor-elect bowed slightly, if not a bit stiffly, and bid Rosalie and her army a fond farewell.

Rosalie's job was now done; she had completed what had seemed only weeks ago an impossible mission: march a ragtag band of suffragettes 175 miles, including detours, to deliver to the Governor-elect the suffrage committee's most heartfelt vision for a more equitable future. She had done it ahead of schedule, and she had done it without sustaining injuries more serious than a few bumps and bruises and far too many blisters.

As they headed back down the hill toward the Hampton Hotel, Rosalie and her pilgrims were in a celebratory mood. In the fight they had been, and in the fight they would remain, unlike another suffragist whose name had been splashed across today's headlines as far away as Toronto. "Albany Reached by Suffragettes," the headlines in that great Canadian city shouted, adding, "Only one of pilgrim sextet failed to finish."[30] The article read, "Mrs. Inez Craven, who was one of the sextet to make the start, dropped out en route." Minus Katherine and Sybil and Jessie, who were too close to journalists to "count" in the eyes of most in the official tally of through-hikers, it left Rosalie, Ida, and Lavinia — the army's "high command"— as the only hikers to tramp the complete distance on foot.

Now the three core members of Rosalie's army, plus Jessie and Gladys, let their newfound momentum carry them down the hill, ecstatic with cheerful talk and breathless recountings of the historic moment they had not just witnessed but made.

CHAPTER 12:
A SUFFRAGETTE NEW YEAR

January 1, Inauguration Day — a new year full of new promise. Rosalie's heart was gladdened, and honored, to spend New Year's in the company of her fellow army officers, who stood beside her now as they watched the Governor known as "Plain Bill" ready himself for the ceremonial trip to the Capitol building for the swearing-in.

All over the great state of New York, New Year's Eve had been an especially wild night full of "rowdyism."[1] A night meant for celebration of all good things to come had instead brought with it the ugliness of five stabbings and what the newspapers called four shooting "scrapes," one of them fatal. Thousands of dollars of plate glass windows had been smashed, and New York City's best had made three hundred arrests. The mayhem of New Year's Eve served as notice of the many powerful forces resident in Rosalie's countrymen and -women — forces long pent-up and needing powerful release.

Despite all the excesses of New Year's Eve, before them strode the soon-to-be Governor, glorying in his trademark simplicity, a man who had insisted on a brief and simple ceremony devoid of any spectacle. All he wanted was an open-air speech to the people.

What's more, the Governor-elect of New York would be stealing a page right from General Rosalie Jones's playbook. Yesterday Rosalie had been thrilled to learn that Plain Bill, true to his name, had declared that he would walk, rather than motor, from the executive mansion to the Capitol, where he would take his oath of office. "I prefer walking," Plain Bill had said, and General Jones couldn't have agreed more.[2] A leader's place was among her or his people, close enough that they could look into their constituents' eyes and feel what lay in their hearts.

Rosalie's army looked on with no small amount of admiration as Plain Bill emerged from the Governor's mansion wearing — what else? — his old gray coat. A well-appointed open carriage had been parked in front of the mansion to entice him, and the carriage attendant now stood holding the door open for the chief executive.[3] Rosalie thrilled as Plain Bill ignored the customary ride and began to march toward the legislature with his unusually long strides, his face drawn in contemplation of the intensity of the moment and the enormity of the task before him. His back was slightly bent, his hands clasped behind it. "Three Cheers for Bill Sulzer!" someone shouted, and another, "No high hat for Sulzer!" It was true, Rosalie noted with delight; in place of the high hat expected of politicians and very important people, Plain Bill had donned, appropriately enough, a slouch hat.

And the homespun Governor had another surprise in store for Rosalie's army. He had personally invited them to the inauguration and asked them to take part in the ceremony by formally presenting to him the suffrage message they had delivered in person a day earlier.[4]

After Rosalie Jones had formally presented the suffrage scroll, after the playing of "The Star-Spangled Banner," and after the swearing of the oath of office (supplemented with the briefest and simplest inauguration speech anyone present could ever remember), Governor William L. Sulzer left the Capitol by the front door and walked out onto the steps to address the thousands who had tried in vain to make their way inside the cramped legislative chambers. Here the new Governor repeated some of his choicest words for the benefit of the appreciative throngs. Wearing his old gray coat, he said:

> I am grateful to the people for their suffrages. I enter
> upon the performance of the duties of the office without a
> promise, except my pledge to all the people to serve them
> faithfully and honestly and to the best of my ability. I am
> free, without entanglements, and shall remain free. No
> influence controls me but the dictates of my conscience
> and my determination to do my duty, day in and day out,
> as I see the right, regardless of consequences. In the future,
> as in the past, I will walk the street called straight, and
> without fear, and without favor I shall execute the laws
> justly and impartially — with malice toward none.[5]

Plain Bill paused briefly throughout his speech to survey the approving crowd.

> Those who know me best know that I stand firmly for certain fundamental principles — for freedom of speech; for the right of lawful assembly, for the freedom of the press; for liberty under law; for civil and religious freedom; for constitutional government; for equality and justice for all… for equal rights to everyone.

When he was through the Governor looked out upon the well-wishers once more, and began to descend the seventy-seven steps that would take him to the street from whence he had come. It seemed a fitting gesture; other governors, as everyone knew, had found ways to avoid the steep steps that ordinary citizens were forced to climb to access the Capitol. Instead, they'd taken back doors and side entrances to arrive at the legislative chambers.

It was true; steps were a thing to be counted, and Rosalie was glad now to descend them at the Governor's side. Small steps, and many of them, were the route by which revolutions happened; the route by which people who disagreed took a step toward one another; the deliberate manner in which well-meaning people invested in their fellow women and men, as the saying goes, one step at a time.

Already writers whose task it was to catalogue the most influential happenings of the past year had singled out the march of the suffragettes as an event that would be discussed for years, if not decades, to come. Writing for *Hearst's Magazine*, Elbert Hubbard claimed that those whom the suffrage hike had touched couldn't help but "talk about it for many moons to come." Summing up the impact of Rosalie's army, he opined, "Anything that gets us out in the storm, out on the open road, and makes us bigger than the elements, is good. Life is a fight — a fight against inertia, against the love of ease, against 'well enough.' And these suffragettes are certainly doing the world good in their invitation to 'fall in, everybody!' Not only will we fall in line and hike with them for a few miles, but we will, in sympathy, fall in love with the cause they represent."[6]

Rosalie Jones and her stalwart officers Ida and Lavinia had taken many steps together for their cause, and they vowed to continue doing so as they descended from the Capitol into a crowd of citizens applauding them, the new Governor, and the promise of a New Year.

Nearly 175 miles the pilgrims had tramped for a just cause, averaging more than fourteen miles per day. Approximately three hundred and seventy thousand steps Rosalie's troops had taken to give substance to a vision. Three hundred and seventy thousand steps toward a goal many men, anti-suffragists, and even their own mothers had told them was impossible, foolhardy, and downright dangerous. Three hundred and seventy thousand steps into the unknown, into the snow, into gunshots and mysterious woods, into hecklers and naysayers and doubters, into open embraces, cheers of support, and tears of gratitude and joy.

The Governor understood something of the great patience such a journey required. Here was a man who moments ago had told the people not what they had wanted to hear — that he would solve all of society's problems overnight — but what was true: "To avoid mistakes I must go slow," he'd said.

And so it was. Rosalie sometimes felt as if she had been born impatient with the status quo, and yet certainly their suffrage hike had not been a quick thing — it had taken weeks of walking and, before that, more time spent in careful planning. It had taken support from people of all walks of life, the kindness of strangers, and provisions stowed away in anticipation of future need.

You could be brave and still be patient and steadfast in your cause, Rosalie must have thought, as she stepped forward into a street overflowing with unbridled hope for the future. You could be a woman of action who refused to wait; you could force the issue; you could force your feet to walk; but you could not force another's heart to change, at least not overnight.

But you could and must, as the Governor himself had said, own your conscience. You could dream of a better, fairer world. You could gather together a small but determined group of friends.

Together you could march into history.

NOTES

This is a work of nonfiction. In an effort to create an accessible account for readers young and old alike, an attempt has been made to avoid overproliferation of duplicative or redundant endnotes, hence the absence here of the term *ibid.* used as academic convention meaning "in the same place as the last term cited." It may be assumed that the source for any material suggesting citation is from "the same place" from the point of first citation though to the first new source cited thereafter. Dialogue and key scenic details in this book have been faithfully gathered from primary sources. Print artifacts from national newspapers of record and national wire services have been preferred throughout; in particular, the author wishes to acknowledge the original reporting done by H. Percy Soule of the *New York Times*, whose reportage served as a "go-to" source for this narrative, as well as the fine reporting of Martin Casey of the *Brooklyn Daily Eagle*, Virginia Hudson of the *New York Press*, and Gertrude Marvin of the *New York Sun*. Meredith N. Stiles of the Associated Press, husband of suffragette marcher Katherine Stiles, also occasionally covered the march; this, and any bias it may have given appearance of having created, may explain the almost complete lack of mention of Katherine Stiles as a suffrage hiker. While nearly all accounts of the suffragette march appear without byline, the identities of the "war correspondent" reporters mentioned above by name are confirmed in the primary record in at least two places, including Jessie Hardy Stubbs's article appearing in volume XLIII, number 52, of *Woman's Journal*, December 28, 1912, and in the description of the pilgrims' and war correspondents' shared Christmas celebration in Hudson, New York, as it appeared in the *Hudson Evening Register* of December 26, 1912.

CHAPTER 1: FIRST STEPS
1. David Dismore, "September 3, 1912: Suffragists Lose in Ohio," Feminist Majority Foundation blog, http://feminist.org/blog/index.php/2014/09/03/september-3-1912-suffragists-lose-in-ohio/
2. "Suffragists Plan Albany Pilgrimage," *New York Times*, December 10, 1912.
3. Louise Bernkow, "The Radical Rich," http://nycitywoman.com/features/radical-rich

4. Natalie Naylor, *Women in Long Island's Past* (Charleston: History Press, 2012), 121.

5. Antonia Petrash, *Long Island and the Woman Suffrage Movement* (Charleston: History Press, 2013), 67–68.

6. George DeWan, "Long Island Our Past," *Newsday,* December 15, 1998.

7. "Suffragists Plan Albany Pilgrimage," *New York Times,* December 10, 1912.

8. American Association for the History of Nursing, "Lavinia Lloyd Dock," https://www.aahn.org/gravesites/dock.html

9. "Women's Suffrage," *The Advertiser* (Adelaide, SA), November 18, 1912, 9. http://trove.nla.gov.au/newspaper/article/5352142]

10. "New States to Lead in Suffrage Parade," *New York Times,* November 9, 1912.

11. "Pilgrims' Peanuts Will Ride in Auto," *New York Times,* December 13, 1912.

12. Ida Husted Harper, ed., *History of Woman Suffrage,* vol. 6. (New York: National American Woman Suffrage Association, 1922), 452.

13. "Pilgrims Tramp to Albany," *Woman's Journal,* December 21, 1912, 401.

14. Quotes and scenic details from the December 12 organizational meeting at suffrage headquarters have been gathered from "Pilgrims' Peanuts Will Ride in Auto," *New York Times,* December 13, 1912.

15. "Doves to Disprove Tales of Militancy," *New York Times,* December 14, 1912.

16. Quotes and scenic details from the December 15 "Preparation Tea" have been gathered from "Suffrage Host off to Albany Today," *New York Times,* December 16, 1912.

17. "Pilgrims Tramp to Albany," *Woman's Journal,* December 21, 1912, 401.

18. "General's Mamma Bound Up State After Daughter," *Brooklyn Daily Eagle,* December 21, 1912.

19. "Pilgrims Tramp to Albany," *Woman's Journal,* December 21, 1912, 401.

20. Quotes from Rosalie and her prospective marchers have been gathered from "'On to Albany!' Cry Spartan Sisters," *Cedar Rapids (IA) Daily Republican,* December 21, 1912.

21. "Can Tight Skirts," *Lowell (MA) Sun,* December 7, 1912.

22. The quotes from Rosalie Jones, Jessie Stubbs, and Ida Craft that close the chapter have been gathered from "'On to Albany!' Cry Spartan Sisters," *Cedar Rapids (IA) Daily Republican,* December 21, 1912.

CHAPTER 2: FORWARD MARCH!

1. "Pilgrims Tramp to Albany," *Woman's Journal,* December 21, 1912, 401.

2. Library of Congress Manuscript Division, Records of the National Woman's Party, https://www.loc.gov/item/mnwp000056/

3. Scenic details of the march as it leaves New York City are gathered from "Six Tired Pilgrims End First Day's Hike," *New York Times,* December 17, 1912.

4. "Suffragettes Begin a Hike of 140 Miles," *Lima (OH) Daily News,* December 16, 1912.

5. Historic Hudson Valley, "Kykuit: The Rockefeller Estate," http://www.hudsonvalley.org/historic-sites/kykuit See also: *Orlando Sentinel* article "Rockefellers to Open Doors of 40-room Mansion to Public," http://articles.orlandosentinel.com/1991-11-02/business/9110310797_1_nelson-rockefeller-rockefeller-brothers-fund-kykuit

6. Information on the attempted assassination of Theodore Roosevelt comes from the National Park Service, "Who Shot T.R.?" Theodore Roosevelt Birthplace National Historic Site, http://www.nps.gov/thrb/learn/historyculture/whoshottr.htm

7. "Roosevelt Says Women Helped," *Woman's Journal,* December 21, 1912, 401

8. "Michigan Boils With Turmoil," *Woman's Journal,* December 21, 1912, 401

9. New York Public Library Rare Books and Manuscript Division, Emily Ford Skeel Papers. "Biographical Note," http://www.nypl.org/sites/default/files/archivalcollections/pdf/skeel.pdf

10. "The Pilgrim Army, Reduced to Five, Bravely Pushes On," *Brooklyn Daily Eagle,* December 17, 1912.

CHAPTER 3: PILGRIMS FOUR

1. Quotes and scenic details in this chapter have been primarily gathered from "Suffrage Pilgrims Down to Four," *New York Times*, December 18, 1912.
2. "Miss Helen Gould Engaged to Marry Railway Official," *Chicago Daily Tribune*, December 16, 1912.
3. "The Pilgrim Army, Reduced to Five, Bravely Pushes On," *Brooklyn Daily Eagle*, December 17, 1912.
4. Jasmine Williams, "Steven Brodie—Daredevil or Hoaxster?" *New York Post*, November 5, 2007, http://nypost.com/2007/11/05/steve-brodie-daredevil-or-hoaxter/ For coverage of Brodie's original alleged jump see "A Leap from the Bridge," *New York Times*, July 24, 1886.
5. Washington Irving, *The Works of Washington Irving* (Philadelphia: Lee and Blanchard, 1840), 333.
6. "Suffrage Pilgrims Down to Four," *New York Times*, December 18, 1912.
7. "The Pilgrim Army, Reduced to Five, Bravely Pushes On," *Brooklyn Daily Eagle*, December 17, 1912.
8. "Suffrage Pilgrims Down to Four," *New York Times*, December 18, 1912.
9. "One Pilgrim Drops Out of March of Suffragists," *Chicago Daily Tribune*, December 18, 1912.
10. "Spirit of Suffrage Pilgrims," *Cincinnati Enquirer*, December 18, 1912.
11. "Suffrage Pilgrims Down to Four," *New York Times*, December 18, 1912.

CHAPTER 4: HEARTACHES AND JAILBREAKS

1. "Suffrage Pilgrims Down to Four," *New York Times*, December 18, 1912.
2. "Suffragists Defy Drizzle and Fog," *New York Times*, December 19, 1912.
3. "Suffrage Hikers in Fog," *Lebanon (PA) Daily News*, December 19, 1912.
4. "Heaviest Fog in Many Years," *Dunkirk (NY) Evening Observer*, December 18, 1912.
5. "Thief Escapes from Sing-Sing," *Kingston (NY) Daily Freeman*, December 19, 1912.
6. "Suffragists Defy Drizzle and Fog," *New York Times*, December 19, 1912.
7. The lyrics for "Blest Be the Tie That Binds" have been gathered from Hymnary.org, http://www.hymnary.org/text/blest_be_the_tie_that_binds
8. "Suffragists Defy Drizzle and Fog," *New York Times*, December 19, 1912.
9. "Gen. Rosalie Jones and Suffrage 'Army' Leaving New York City," *Sandusky Star Journal*, December 20, 1912.
10. "Inez Carven Wasn't Wanted on March," *Brooklyn Daily Eagle*, December 19, 1912.
11. "The Militant Suffragette," *Hearst's Magazine* 23 (1913): 807

CHAPTER 5: EVEN GENERALS HAVE MOTHERS

1. "Pilgrims March Bravely Onward," *Woman's Journal*, December 28, 1912.
2. "Calls Back General of Suffrage Army," *New York Times*, December 21, 1912.
3. "Hikers out of Fog, Battle with the Wind," *New York Times*, December 20, 1912.
4. "Suffrage Army Plods in Storm," *Chicago Daily Tribune*, December 20, 1912.
5. United Press Assocations, *Daily Capital (OR) Journal*, December 20, 1912.
6. "Suffrage Army Plods in Storm," *Chicago Daily Tribune*, December 20,1912.
7. "Calls Back General of Suffrage Army," *New York Times*, December 21, 1912.
8. United Press Associations, *Daily Capital (OR) Journal*, December 20, 1912.
9. "Walkers Tired: Original Sixty Now Only Four," *Waterloo (IA) Evening Courier*, December 20, 1912.
10. "Calls Back General of Suffrage Army," *New York Times*, December 21, 1912.
11. "Double Crime Due to Pride," *Brooklyn Daily Eagle*, December 21, 1912.
12. "Girl of 15 Secretly Wed," *Brooklyn Daily Eagle*, December 17, 1912.
13. "On Their Way: Remnant of Suffragette Pilgrimage Sticking To It," *Kokomo (IN) Tribune*, December 21, 1912.

14. "'Albany or Bust' Is Cry of Suffragettes," *Allegany County (NY) Reporter*, December 24, 1912.

15. "Calls Back General of Suffrage Army," *New York Times*, December 21, 1912.

16. "'Albany or Bust' Is Cry of Suffragettes," *Allegany County (NY) Reporter*, December 24, 1912.

17. "Gen. Jones' Mama Is Going to Bring Her Back Home—If!" *Evening-World* (NY), December 21, 1912.

18. "Spoil Mails in London," *Chicago Daily Tribune*, December 23, 1912.

19. "Suffragette Hikers Reach Poughkeepsie," *Brooklyn Daily Eagle*, December 21, 1912.

CHAPTER 6: LETTERS FROM THE FRONT

1. "Girls Desert Mill to Follow Hikers," *New York Times*, December 22, 1912.

2. "Suffragette Hikers Reach Poughkeepsie," *Brooklyn Daily Eagle*, December 21, 1912.

3. "General's Mamma Bound Up State After Daughter," *Brooklyn Daily Eagle*, December 21, 1912.

4. "Girls Desert Mill to Follow Hikers," *New York Times*, December 21, 1912.

5. "Wellesleyites Welcome Stork," *Cedar Rapids (IA) Daily Republican*, December 21, 1912.

6. "Girls Desert Mill to Follow Hikers," *New York Times*, December 21, 1912.

7. "General's Mamma Bound Up State After Daughter," *Brooklyn Daily Eagle*, December 21, 1912

8. "Suffragette Hikers Reach Poughkeepsie," *Brooklyn Daily Eagle*, December 21, 1912.

9. "Girls Desert Mill to Follow Hikers," *New York Times*, December 21, 1912.

10. "General's Mamma Bound Up State After Daughter," *Brooklyn Daily Eagle*, December 21, 1912.

11. "Suffragette Hikers Reach Poughkeepsie," *Brooklyn Daily Eagle*, December 21, 1912.

12. "General's Mamma Bound Up State After Daughter," *Brooklyn Daily Eagle*, December 21, 1912.

13. "Suffragette Hikers Reach Poughkeepsie," *Brooklyn Daily Eagle*, December 21, 1912.

14. "General's Mamma Bound Up State After Daughter," *Brooklyn Daily Eagle*, December 21, 1912.

15. "New York Suffragists Hike 16 Miles on Sabbath," *Chicago Daily Tribune*, December 23, 1912.

16. "Romance Stirs Suffrage Ranks," *Middletown (NY) Daily Times-Press*, December 26, 1912.

17. "Suffragists Hunt a Place to Sleep," *New York Times*, December 24, 1912.

18. "Pilgrims March Bravely Onward," *Woman's Journal*, December 28, 1912.

CHAPTER 7: LIVES OF THE RICH AND FAMOUS

1. "Army Reaches Rhinebeck," *Boston Post*, December 23, 1912.

2. "Suffragist Pilgrims Meet Vincent Astor," *New York Times*, December 23, 1912.

3. "Romance Thrills Suffragettes on March to Albany," *New York Press*, December 26, 1912.

4. "'On to Washington' Next Pilgrim Cry," *Brooklyn Daily Eagle*, December 26, 1912.

5. "Suffragist Pilgrims Meet Vincent Astor," *New York Times*, December 23, 1912.

6. Charles Eliot Fitch, *Encyclopedia of Biography of New York: A Life Record of Men and Women…* vol. 1. (Boston: American Historical Society, n.d.), http://www.ebooksread.com/authors-eng/charles-e-charles-elliott-fitch/encyclopedia-of-biography-of-new-york-a-life-record-of-men-and-women-whose-ster-cti/page-12-encyclopedia-of-biography-of-new-york-a-life-record-of-men-and-women-whose-ster-cti.shtml

7. "Suffragist Pilgrims Meet Vincent Astor," *New York Times*, December 23, 1912.

8. Geoffrey C. Ward, *Before the Trumpet: Young Franklin Roosevelt 1882-1905* (New York: Vintage, 1985).

9. "Suffragist Pilgrims Meet Vincent Astor," *New York Times*, December 23, 1912.

10. "Suffragist Pilgrims Meet Vincent Astor," *New York Times*, December 23, 1912.

11. *Encyclopedia Titanica*, "Colonel John Jacob Astor," http://www.encyclopedia-titanica.org/titanic-victim/john-jacob-astor.html

12. "Vincent Astor Dies In His Home at 67," *New York Times*, February 4, 1959.

13. New York Social Diary, "An Astor Legacy Fit for Celebrating…," July 8, 2010, http://www.newyorksocialdiary.com/social-diary/2010/an-astor-legacy-fit-for-celebrating-chelsea-clintons-wedding

14. "Suffragist Pilgrims Meet Vincent Astor," *New York Times*, December 23, 1912.

CHAPTER 8: A PILGRIM'S CHRISTMAS

1. "Suffragists March 22 Miles in the Snow," *New York Times*, December 25, 1912.
2. "Calls Back General of Suffrage Army," *New York Times*, December 21, 1912.
3. "Suffragists Hunt a Place to Sleep," *New York Times,* December 24, 1912.
4. "Suffragists Plod 24 Miles," *Chicago Daily Tribune*, December 25, 1912.
5. "Suffragists Hunt a Place to Sleep," *New York Times,* December 24, 1912.
6. "Suffragists Plod 24 Miles," *Chicago Daily Tribune*, December 25, 1912.
7. "Suffragists March 22 Miles in the Snow," *New York Times,* December 25, 1912.
8. "Hot Chase for Rockefeller," *New York Times*, December 19, 1912. For information on Rockefeller's preferred disguises, see also: "Special to the New York Times," *New York Times*, December 28, 1912.
9. "Suffragists March 22 Miles in the Snow," *New York Times*, December 25, 1912.
10. "Suffragist Army Marches On," *New York Sun*, December 28 1912.
11. "Suffragists March 22 Miles in the Snow," *New York Times,* December 25, 1912.
12. "Suffragists Plod 24 Miles," *Chicago Daily Tribune*, December 25, 1912.
13. "Automobile Bandits," *Hutchinson (KS) News*, December 21, 1912.
14. "Suffragists March 22 Miles in the Snow," *New York Times,* December 25, 1912.
15. Advertisement, *Cedar Rapids (IA) Daily Republican*, December 21, 1912.
16. Advertisement, *Evening-World* (NY), December 21, 1912.
17. "Santa Claus Has Ban on Diamonds," *Des Moines (IA) News*, December 4, 1912.
18. "Many Urgent Cases Left For Do-Something Club," *Brooklyn Daily Eagle*, December 22, 1912.
19. Associated Press, "Blistered Feet No Bar to Hike," *Gazette and Bulletin* (PA), December 26, 1912.
20. "Suffragists Plod 24 Miles," *Chicago Daily Tribune*, December 25, 1912.
21. "General Jones Dons Skates to Rest Blisters," *San Francisco Call,* December 26, 1912.
22. "Romance Thrills Suffragettes on March to Albany," *New York Press*, December 26, 1912.
23. Associated Press, "Blistered Feet No Bar to Hike," *Gazette and Bulletin* (PA), December 26, 1912.
24. "Suffragists Plod 24 Miles," *Chicago Daily Tribune*, December 25, 1912.
25. "Wedding in Sight for Suffrage Army," *New York Times*, December 26, 1912.
26. Associated Press, "Blistered Feet No Bar to Hike," *Gazette and Bulletin* (PA), December 26, 1912.
27. "Romance Thrills Suffragettes on March to Albany," *New York Press*, December 26, 1912.
28. "Romance Stirs Suffrage Ranks," *Middletown (NY) Daily Times-Press*, December 26, 1912.
29. *Encyclopedia Titanica,* "Miss Gretchen Fiske Longley," http://www.encyclopedia-titanica.org/titanic-survivor/gretchen-fiske-longley.html
30. "Wedding in Sight for Suffrage Army," *New York Times*, December 26, 1912.
31. "Romance Thrills Suffragettes on March to Albany," *New York Press*, December 26, 1912.
32. "Wedding in Sight for Suffrage Army," *New York Times*, December 26, 1912.
33. "'On to Washington' Next Pilgrim Cry," *Brooklyn Daily Eagle*, December 26, 1912.
34. "Romance Thrills Suffragettes on March to Albany," *New York Press*, December 26, 1912.

CHAPTER 9: JINGLE BELLS AND SHOTGUN SHELLS

1. Anna Cadogan Etz, "They Did It," *Woman's Journal*, December 28, 1913.
2. "Romance Stirs Suffrage Ranks," *Middletown (NY) Daily Times Press*, December 26, 1912.
3. "'On to Washington' Next Pilgrim Cry," *Brooklyn Daily Eagle*, December 26, 1912.
4. "Suffragists Brave Both Guns and Snow," *New York Times*, December 26, 1912.
5. "Suffragettes Near Albany," *Medina (NY) Daily Journal*, December 27, 1912.
6. "Left Stockport This Morning," *Hudson (NY) Evening Register*, December 27, 1912.
7. "Suffragettes Attack Railroad Companies," *Colorado Springs-Gazette*, December 27, 1912.
8. "Can't Find Rockefeller…" *The (NY) Daily Herald,* December 27, 1912.
9. "Suffrage Army Thrown Out of Auto Into Mud," *New York Sun*, December 28, 1912.
10. "Suffrage Hikers Near Death When the Chainless Tires of Their Auto Skidded," *New York Times*, December 29, 1912.

11. Margaret Watts De Peyster, "Auto Accident All But Stops Suffrage Army," *San Francisco Call*, December 28, 1912.

12. "Suffrage Hikers Near Death When the Chainless Tires of Their Auto Skidded," *New York Times*, December 29, 1912.

13. "Hikers Near Goal. Women Have Narrow Escape from Injury When Auto Skids on 20-foot Embankment," *Logansport (IN) Pharos*, December 28, 1912.

14. "Suffrage Army Thrown Out of Auto Into Mud," *New York Sun*, December 28, 1912.

15. Margaret Watts De Peyster, "Auto Accident All But Stops Suffrage Army," *San Francisco Call*, December 28, 1912.

16. "Suffrage Army Thrown Out of Auto Into Mud," *New York Sun*, December 28, 1912.

17. Margaret Watts De Peyster, "Auto Accident All But Stops Suffrage Army," *San Francisco Call*, December 28, 1912.

18. "Pilgrimettes Near End of Their Journey," *Ithaca (NY) Evening News*, December 28, 1912.

19. Margaret Watts De Peyster, "Auto Accident All But Stops Suffrage Army," *San Francisco Call*. December 28, 1912.

CHAPTER 10: ALBANY OR BUST!

1. "Suffragists Finish March to Albany," *New York Times*, December 29, 1912.

2. "Suffrage Army Thrown Out of Auto Into Mud," *New York Sun*, December 28, 1912.

3. "Suffragists Finish March to Albany," *New York Times*, December 29, 1912.

4. "Suffrage Army Thrown Out of Auto Into Mud," *New York Sun*, December 28, 1912.

5. Lyrics from *Libretti Tannhäuser* have been gathered from http://www.rwagner.net/libretti/tannhauser/e-tannh-a3s1.html

6. "Suffragists Finish March to Albany," *New York Times*, December 29, 1912.

7. "Suffrage Army at End of Hike," *Des Moines (IA) News*, December 29, 1912.

8. "Sulzer Swears Aid to Cause," *Woman's Journal*, January 4, 1913.

9. "Suffrage Army Is at Albany," *Boston Sunday Post*, December 29, 1912.

10. "Sulzer Swears Aid to Cause," *Woman's Journal*, January 4, 1913.

11. "Little Band of Pilgrims Arrive Two Days Ahead of Their Schedule," *Syracuse (NY) Herald*, December 29, 1912.

12. "Suffragists Finish March to Albany," *New York Times*, December 29, 1912.

13. Ida Husted Harper, ed., *History of Woman Suffrage*, vol. 6. (New York: National American Woman Suffrage Association, 1922), 452.

14. "Suffrage Army at End of Hike," *Des Moines (IA) News*, December 29, 1912.

15. "Suffragists Finish March to Albany," *New York Times*, December 29, 1912.

16. "Suffrage Army Is at Albany," *Boston Sunday Post*, December 29, 1912.

CHAPTER 11: IN THE FIGHT!

1. "Suffrage Army Spends Day of Rest at Albany," *San Francisco Call*, December 30, 1912.

2. "Sulzer Swears to Aid to Cause," *Woman's Journal*, January 4, 1913.

3. "Suffragist Scouts Out to Sight Sulzer," *New York Times*, December 30, 1912.

4. All headlines in this sentence are quoted from the *Logansport (IN) Pharos*, December 28, 1912.

5. This headline, "Deaf Mute Stabs Woman to Death When She Scorns Him," and the headlines referenced immediately after, including "Former 'Stork' Mayor to Introduce Bachelor Bill," "Ask Grand Jury to Investigate the Work of Girls," and "Twenty Cents a Day What 17,000 Have for Existence." appeared on Page One of the *Des Moines (IA) News*, December 29, 1912.

6. "Mr. Carnegie Will Give 25,000,000 More to Charities," *Logansport (IN) Pharos*, December 28, 1912.

7. "William Rockefeller is Found," *The Daily Journal (Stevens Point, WI)*, December 30, 1912. For information on Rockefeller's preferred disguises, see also: "Special to the New York Times," *New York Times*, December 28, 1912.

8. "Girl Taken As Firebug," *Logansport (IN) Pharos*, December 28, 1912.

9. "Suffrage Hikers Were Near Death When the Chainless Tires of their Auto Skidded," *New York Times*, December 27, 1912.

10. "Suffragists Finish March to Albany," *New York Times,* December 29, 1912.

11. Suffrage Army Spends Day of Rest at Albany," *San Francisco Call*, December 30, 1912.

12. "Suffragists Finish March to Albany," *New York Times,* December 29, 1912.

13. "Suffragist Scouts Out to Sight Sulzer," *New York Times*, December 30, 1912.

14. "Suffrage Army Is Denounced by Bishop of Albany," *New York Press*, December 30, 1912.

15. "'Gen.' De Forest Beats 'Gen.' Jones in Seeing Sulzer," *New York Sun,* December 29, 1912.

16. Jessie Hardy Stubbs, "In the Fight!" *Woman's Journal*, January 4, 1913.

17. "Mrs. Stubbs Gets Some Joyful News," *Brooklyn Daily Eagle*, December 30, 1912.

18. "Watching for Sulzer," *New York Times*, December 31, 1912.

19. "Mrs. Stubbs Gets Some Joyful News," *Brooklyn Daily Eagle*, December 30, 1912.

20. "Sulzer Swears Aid to Cause," *Woman's Journal*, January 4, 1913.

21. "Suffrage Army Is Denounced by Bishop of Albany," *New York Press*, December 30, 1912.

22. "Pilgrims' Sentries Watch for Sulzer," *Brooklyn Daily Eagle*, December 30, 1912.

23. "Women Erred on Name," *New York Times*, December 31, 1912.

24. "Sulzer Will Walk to Capitol Today," *New York Times,* January 1, 1913.

25. "Sulzer Warns Tammany Off," *New York Times*, December 31, 1912.

26. "Sulzer to Aid Suffragists," *New York Sun,* December 31, 1912.

27. "Women Erred on Name," *New York Times*, December 31, 1912.

28. "Sulzer to Aid Suffragists," *New York Sun*, December 31, 1912.

29. "Women Erred on Name," *New York Times*, December 31, 1912.

30. "Albany Reached by Suffragettes," *Toronto World*, December 30, 1912.

CHAPTER 12: A SUFFRAGETTE NEW YEAR

1. "Eastern Cities Show Rowdyism," *Berkeley (CA) Daily Gazette*, January 1, 1913.

2. "Sulzer Will Walk to Capitol Today," *New York Times*, January 1, 1913.

3. "Sulzer Is Installed in Plain Ceremony," *New York Times*, January 2, 1913

4. "N. Y. Inaugurates Sulzer Governor," *Berkeley (CA) Daily Gazette*, January 1, 1913.

5. "Sulzer Is Installed in Plain Ceremony," *New York Times*, January 2, 1913.

6. Hubbard, Elbert, "Suffrage Hike to Albany," *Hearst's Magazine* 23 (1913): 312.

Jessie Hardy Stubbs and "General" Rosalie Gardiner Jones.